Ancient Valour

*The Queen's York Rangers
on Operations,
from 1756 to Present*

Back Cover Images:

<u>First Row</u>: Metal Crescent Moon, Queen's Rangers. Shako Plate, Incorporated Militia of Upper Canada. Officers' Cap Badge, 12th Regiment, York Rangers. NCM Cap Badge, 12th Regiment, York Rangers.

<u>Second Row</u>: 20th Bn, CEF. Interim Collar Badge, 20th Bn CEF. York Rangers. Final badge, 20th Bn, CEF.

<u>Third Row</u>: Officers' Cap Badge, 20th Bn, CEF. 35th Bn, CEF. 127th Bn, CEF. 220th Bn. CEF.

<u>Fourth Row</u>: Formation Patch, 20th Bn, CEF. Combat Cap Badge, Queen's York Rangers. 2nd Design, Combat Cap Badge, Queen's York Rangers. Unofficial OPFOR Cap Badge, Queen's York Rangers.

<u>Fifth Row</u>: Officers' Cap Badge, King's Crown, Queen's York Rangers. NCM Cap Badge, Queen's York Rangers.

Editors: Phil Halton, Chris Wattie
Researchers: Phil Halton, Jeremy Hood
Cover Design: Leif Halton, Phil Halton

ISBN: 978-1-9994613-4-8
ISBN: 978-1-9994613-5-5 (e-book)

DEDICATION

This anthology is dedicated to all the men
and women whose service has made the
Rangers as feared and famous a Regiment
as it is today.

Pristinae Virtutis Memor

Table of Contents

Preface

Preface

A Regiment is a remarkable thing.

It is not a static entity that can be captured on an organization chart – it is an organic, living thing. Although humans perceive the organization in relation to ourselves, in the moment in time when we observe it, this is only a glimpse of its existence. As members of the unit come and go, even over a period of hundreds of years, the organism that is the Regiment carries on without interruption. Therefore, the unit that exists today does not just perpetuate or honour or remember its history. It continues to live it in a manner that mere humans cannot.

This anthology of first-person accounts of Rangers on operations is not really about any one contributor as an individual. It is intended instead as a public recognition of the fact that the Regiment continues. It lives on. It sheds its skin, changes it name and its outward appearance, but afterwards remains the same Regiment as it was before. It remains solidly rooted in the past while stretching outward into the unknown future.

What allows a Regiment to be have the resiliency to survive through centuries of service while still retaining its essential character is the incredibly dense and tightly woven fabric of relationships that give it cohesion on a daily basis. These relationships connect all of the members of the Regimental family together, including those serving today and those who served in the past. This tapestry of people forms the foundation of the Regiment, and gives it strength.

The soldiers of this Regiment are a remarkable group of people, embodying the ideal of the citizen-soldier since its inception in 1756. Despite everything that has been written about the focus on "me" that is allegedly prevalent in Canadian society today, the members of the Queen's York Rangers today have made the commitment to serve their country and their community in their spare time, much as members of the Regiment have done for hundreds of years. This focus on service to our communities is an essential quality of the Regiment that has endured over centuries.

This anthology is a celebration of the strength of the fabric of the Regimental family, both as it is today and as it will be in the future. Reading these personal accounts of service in operations, we see both what has changed and what has stayed the same, and we are able to acknowledge that, whatever future changes may occur, that the Queen's York Rangers remain strong and ready to serve our country, in peace and in war.

The Seven Years War

The first global war that the world had seen was fought from 1756 to 1763, in Europe, India and in America, as well as on the seas that stretched between them. British and French interests clashed in North America, drawing in the continent's Indigenous peoples as well. When it ended, the French had lost their empire in North America, and a new way of warfare had entered the military imagination, "la petite guerre," whose pre-eminent practitioners were the Rangers.

Lieutenant Colonel Robert Rogers

Robert Rogers is one of the most famous frontiersmen in American history, first raising a unit of Rangers for service against the French and their Indian allies in 1756. He had been engaged in warfare since he was a teenager, raiding and countering raids around his family home in New Hampshire. He served as an officer in the British Army during the French and Indian War and again during the American Revolution. Aside from being a soldier, he was an author, playwright, land speculator, Royal Governor of Michilimackinac, fur trader, gambler, and forger, dying penniless in London, UK in 1795.

March 10, 1758

Soon after Captain Putnam's return, in consequence of positive orders from Colonel Haviland, I this day began a march from Fort Edward for the neighbourhood of Carillon, not with a party of 400 men, as first given out, but of 180 men only, officers included, one Captain, one Lieutenant, and one Ensign, and three volunteers, viz. Mess Creed, Kent and Wrightson, one sergeant, and one private, all volunteers of the 27th Regiment, and a detachment from the four companies of Rangers, quartered on the Island near Fort Edward, viz Captain Bulkley, Lieutenants Philips, Moore,

Crafton, Campbell and Pottinger, Ensigns Ross, Wait, McDonald and White, and 162 private men.

I acknowledge I entered upon this service, and viewed this small detachment of brave men march out, with no little concern and uneasiness of mind; for as there was the greatest reason to suspect, that the French were, by the prisoner and the deserter above mentioned, fully informed of the design of sending me out upon Putnam's return: what could I think! To see my party, instead of being strengthened and augmented, reduced to less than half the number at first proposed. I must confess it appeared to me (ignorant and unskilled as I was then in politics and the arts of war incomprehensible; but my commander doubtless had his reasons, and is able to vindicate his own conduct.

We marched to the half-way brook, in the road leading to Lake George, and there encamped the first night.

The 11th we proceeded as far as the first Narrows on Lake George, and encamped that evening on the east-side of the lake; and after dark, I sent a party three miles further down, to see if the enemy might be coming towards our forts, but they returned without discovering any. We were however out on our guard, and kept parties walking on the lake all night, besides sentries at all necessary paces on the land.

The 12th we marched from our encampment at sunrise, and having distanced it about three miles, I saw a dog running across the lake, whereupon I sent a detachment to reconnoitre the island, thinking the Indians might have laid in ambush there for us; but no such could be discovered; upon which I thought it expedient to put to shore, and lay by till night to prevent any party from descrying us on the lake, from hills, or otherwise. We halted at a place called Sabbath-day Point, on the westside of the lake, and sent out parties to look down the lake with perspective glasses, which we had for that purpose.

As soon as it was dark we proceeded down the lake. I sent Lieutenant Philips with fifteen men, as an advanced guard, some of whom went before him on skates, while Ensign Ross flanked us on the left under the west shore, near which we kept the main body, marching as close as

4

possible, to prevent separation, it being a very dark night. In this manner we continued our march till within eight miles of the French advanced guards, when Lieutenant Philips sent a man on skates back to me, to desire me to halt; upon which I ordered my own men to squat down upon the ice.

Mr. Philips soon came to me himself, leaving his party to look out, and said, he imagined that he had discovered a fire on the east shore, but was not certain; upon which I sent with him Ensign White, to make further discovery. In about an hour they returned, fully persuaded that a party of the enemy was encamped there. I then called in the advanced guard, and flanking party, and marched on to the west-shore, where, in a thicket, we hid our sleighs and packs, leaving a small guard with them, and with the remainder I marched to attack the enemy's encampment, if there was any; but when we came near the place, no fires were to be seen, which made us conclude that we had mistaken some bleach patches of snow, or pieces of rotten wood, for fire (which in the night, at a distance, resembles it) whereupon we returned to our packs, and there lay the remainder of the night without fire.

The 13th, in the morning, I deliberated with the officers how to proceed, who were unanimously of opinion, that it was best to go by land in snow-shoes, lest the enemy should discover us on the lake; we accordingly continued our march on the west-side, keeping on the back of the mountains that overlooked the French advanced guards.

At twelve of the clock we halted two miles west of those guards, and there refreshed ourselves till three, that the day-scout from the fort might be returned home before we advanced; intending at night to ambuscade some of their roads, in order to trepan them in the morning. We then marched in two divisions, the one headed by Captain Bulkley, the other by myself: Ensigns White and Wait had the rear-guard, the other officers were posted properly in each division, having a rivulet at a small distance on our left; and a steep mountain on our right. We kept close to the mountain, that the advanced guard might better observe the rivulet, on the ice of which I imagined they would travel if out, as snow was four feet deep, and very bad travelling on snow-shoes.

In this manner we marched a mile and a half, when our advanced guard informed me of the enemy being in their view; and soon after, that they had ascertained their number to be ninety-six, chiefly Indians.

We immediately laid down our packs, and prepare for the battle, supposing these to be the whole number or main body of the enemy, who were marching on our left up the rivulet, upon the ice. I ordered Ensign McDonald to the command of the advanced guard, which, as we faced to the left, made a flanking party to our right. We marched to within a few yards of the bank, which was higher than the ground we occupied; and observing the ground gradually to descend from the bank of the rivulet to the foot of the mountain, we extended our party along the bank, far enough to command the whole of the enemy's at once; we waited till their front was nearly opposite to our left wing, when I fired a gun, as a signal for a general discharge upon them; whereupon we gave them the first fire, which killed above forty Indians; the rest retreated, and were pursued by about one half of our people.

I now imagined the enemy totally defeated, and ordered Ensign McDonald to head the flying remains of them, that none might escape; but we soon found our mistake, and that the party we had attacked were only their advanced guard, their main body coming up, consisted of 600 more, Canadians and Indians; upon which I ordered our people to retreat to their own ground, which we gained at the expense of fifty mean killed; the remainder I rallied, and drew up in pretty good order, where they fought with such intrepidity and bravery as obliged the enemy (tho' seven to one in number) to retreat a second time; but we not being in a condition to pursue them, they rallied again, and recovered their ground, and warmly pushed us in front and both wings, while the mountain defended our rear; but they were so warmly received, that their flanking parties soon retreated to their main body with considerable loss.

This threw the whole again into disorder, and they retreated a third time; but our number being now too far reduced to take advantage of their disorder, they rallied again, and made a fresh attack upon us.

About this time we discovered 200 Indians going up the mountain on our right, as we supposed, to get possession of the rising ground, and attack our rear; to prevent which I sent Lieutenant Philips, with eighteen men, to gain the first possession, and beat them back,; which he did: and being suspicious that the enemy would go round on our left, and take possession of the other part of the hill, I sent Lieutenant Crafton, with fifteen men, to prevent them there; and soon after desired two gentlemen, who were volunteers in the party, with a few men, to go and support him, which they did with great bravery.

The enemy pushed us so close in front, that the parties were not more than twenty yards asunder in general, and sometimes intermixed with each other. The fire continued almost constant for an hour and a half from beginning of the attack, in which time we lost eight officers, and more than100 private men killed on the spot.

We were a last obliged to break, and I with about twenty men ran up the hill to Philips and Crafton, where we stopped and fired on the Indians, who were eagerly pushing us, with numbers that we could not withstand.

Lieutenant Philips being surrounded by 300 Indians, was at this time capitulating for himself and party, on the other part of the hill. He spoke to me, and said if the enemy would give them good quarters, he thought it best to surrender, otherwise that we would fight while he had one man left to fire a gun.

I now thought it most prudent to retreat, and bring off with me as many of my party as I possibly could, which I immediately did; the Indians closely pursuing us at the same time, took several prisoners. We came to Lake George in the evening, where we found several wounded men, whom we took with us to the place where we had left our sleds, from whence I sent an express to Fort Edward, desiring Mr. Haviland to send a party to meet us, and assist in bringing in the wounded; with the remainder I tarried there the whole night, without fire or blankets, and in the morning we proceeded up the lake, and met with Captain Stark at Hoop Island, six miles north from Fort William-Henry, and encamped there that night; the next day being the 15th, in the evening, we arrived at Fort Edward.

The number of enemy was about 700, 600 of which were Indians. By the best account we could get, we killed 150 of them, and wounded as many more. I will not pretend to determine what we should have done had we been 400 or more strong; but I am obliged to say of those brave men who attended me (most of whom are now no more) both officers and soldiers in their respective stations behaved with uncommon resolution and courage; nor do I know an instance during the whole action in which I can justly impeach the prudence or good conduct of any one of them.

The American Revolutionary War

From 1775 to 1783, the Thirteen Colonies and their French Allies fought for independence from Great Britain. Sometimes forgotten is that some of the fiercest fighting was done between Americans – loyalists and rebels – splitting the population and creating grievances that would erupt again thirty years later. One of the finest infantry units raised in the Colony as part of the British Army were the Queen's Rangers, or 1st American Regiment.

Lieutenant General John Graves Simcoe

John Graves Simcoe was commissioned into the 35th Regiment of Foot in 1770. He commanded the Queen's Rangers from 1777 to 1781, and again from 1792 to 1796. Besides being a soldier, he was also a Member of Parliament, the Lieutenant Governor of Upper Canada, and the Governor of Haiti. He died while en route to take office as the Commander-in-Chief of India.

[Note: Simcoe wrote his journal for publication in the third person, which is excerpted here.]

Lt. Col. Simcoe, on the 9th of June, was detached with his cavalry to destroy some tobacco in the warehouses, on the northern bank of the Fluvana: he passed at the lowest ford, and proceeding to the Seven islands, destroyed one hundred and fifty barrels of gunpowder and burnt all the tobacco in the warehouses on the river fide, returning with some rebel militia whom he had surprized and made prisoners. The army remained in this district 'till the thirteenth of June; and the cavalry of the Queen's Rangers made several patrols, particularly one to Bird's ordinary, at midnight, where, it was understood, the Marquis de la Fayette, with his forces, had arrived. It appeared, however, that they were at a great distance, so that the army moved towards Richmond, the Queen's Rangers forming the rear guard. The 71st Regiment here left the Rangers, the two corps had acted with the utmost harmony together, and Lt. Col. Simcoe remembers, with great satisfaction, the expressions of goodwill and regret which both the officers and soldiers of that distinguished regiment made use of, when they quitted his command.

Earl Cornwallis arrived at Richmond the 16th of June. On the 17th, Lt. Col. Simcoe was detached with some infantry and his cavalry, to pass the James river, near Henric's Court-house, which he did the next morning, to facilitate the passage of the boats with convalescents up to Richmond, and to clear the southern banks of the James river of any parties of militia who might be stationed to annoy them. The detachment re-crossed the river on the night of the 19th, from Manchester to Richmond, and Capt. Ewald, with the jaegers, joined the Queen's Rangers.

On the 20th it being reported that the enemy had a flying corps, all mounted, under Gen. Muhlenberg, and consisting of twelve hundred men, Lt. Col. Simcoe was directed to patrol for intelligence; he marched with forty cavalry (but considering this a service of particular danger) with the utmost caution. He quitted the road and marched through the woods, as nearly parallel to it as the enclosures, which had been cleared, would admit.

After a march of a few miles, to his great satisfaction, he discovered a flag of truce, of the enemy and he was certain, that according to their custom, some of them would be found in its rear. Lt. Spencer was therefore detached with a small party to get beyond them upon the road, which he effected, and found himself in the rear of a party of twenty men; but the woods on his right being open, though Lt. Lawler supported him in front, one officer and two or three men only were taken.

Lt. Col. Simcoe immediately returned, having procured from the prisoners every requisite intelligence. The army marched, on the 21st of June, to Bottom-bridge, and on the 22d to New Kent Courthouse; the Queen's Rangers, who made the rear with the jaegers, lay near two miles on the left of the army. Lt. Col. Simcoe was ordered to march the next day towards the Chickahominy, where it was supposed there was a foundry, and some boats; these he was to destroy, to collect all the cattle he could find in the country, and proceed to Williamsburg and Lord Cornwallis expressly told him, that he might, in these operations, safely stay two or three days behind the army, who were to be at Williamsburg on the 25th of June.

Lt. Col. Simcoe marched early in the morning of the 24th, consuming a quantity of Indian corn, which had been collected by the enemy's commissary, at the house where they were headquartered; he found little or nothing to destroy on the Chickahominy, and halted that night at Dandrige's, as Earl Cornwallis did in the neighbourhood of Bird's ordinary.

The bridge over the Diescung creek (a branch of the Chickahominy) had been broken down; this was three miles in the rear of the detachment, and Lt. Col. Simcoe would have passed it that night, so diffident was he of his security, had not the men been too much fatigued with their march, to be employed in so laborious a talk as the repair of this bridge was understood to be.

The next morning, at day break, the detachment arrived there; it had been carelessly destroyed, and was, by anxious and laborious exertion, repaired sufficiently to pass over. Lt. Col. Simcoe then destroyed it most effectually, and marched on to Cooper's mills on the 25th, near twenty miles from Williamsburg, where Earl Cornwallis arrived in the course of the day. Lord Cornwallis's wagons had been at the mills the day before, and taken from thence all the flour they contained, so that it was difficult to get subsistence. Lt. Col. Simcoe felt his situation to be a very anxious one; he had not the smallest information of the enemy's movements, whom he knew to be active and enterprising; to have been lately joined by Gen. Wayne; and, that it was their obvious policy, to follow Earl Cornwallis as far towards the neck of Williamsburg as with safety they could, and to take any little advantage which they could magnify in their newspapers. He had received no advices from Earl Cornwallis, whose general intelligence he knew to be very bad; and he and Major

Armstrong agreed with Capt. Ewald, that the slightest reliance was not to be placed on any patrols from his Lordship's army. The next advantage, to receiving good intelligence, is to deceive the enemy with that which is false. Lt. Col. Simcoe could not procure any confidential person to go to M. de la Fayette's camp; he therefore promised a great reward to a man, whom he knew to be a rebel, to go thither, with express injunctions to return to him by six or seven o'clock, at the farthest, the next morning, at which time he said he should march. The man accordingly set out towards night; and, at two o'clock in the morning. Major Armstrong with the jaegers, infantry and cannon, was on his march to Spencer's ordinary, on the forks of the road between Williamsburg and Jamestown: there he was to halt 'till the cavalry joined him, and then the whole, with the convoy of cattle, which Capt. Branson, with some North Carolina Loyalists, had been employed to collect, was to proceed to Williamsburg.

Lt. Col. Simcoe, with the cavalry, was under arms at the time his infantry marched, and ready to proceed whenever Captain Branson thought there was light sufficient to drive the cattle, and to collect whatever might be met with on the road; the cavalry did not leave their camp 'till three o'clock. On approaching Spencer's ordinary, Lt. Col. Simcoe ordered the fences to be thrown down, and rode into the open ground upon the right, observing it, as was his custom, and remarking, to the officers with him, "that it was an admirable place for the chicanery of action." Lt. Lawler had been previously sent to direct the infantry to move onward to Williamsburg, when Major Armstrong returning with him, informed Lt. Col. Simcoe that there were near a hundred head of cattle in the neighbourhood; but that he waited 'till the drivers arrived to spare the infantry from that fatigue.

Capt. Branson, with his people, went to collect them; and Capt. Shank, who commanded the cavalry, was directed to feed his horses at Lee's farm, and Lt. Colonel Simcoe accompanied Major Armstrong to the infantry. The highland Company of the Queen's Rangers had been paused in the wood, by the side of the road, as a piquet; a shot or two from their sentinels gave an alarm, and Lt. Col. Simcoe galloping across the field, towards the wood, saw Capt. Shank in pursuit of the enemy's cavalry. They had passed through the fences which had been pulled down, as before mentioned, so that, unperceived by the highlanders, they arrived at Lee's farm, in pursuit of the people who were collecting the cattle.

Trumpeter Barney, who had been stationed as a vidette, gave the alarm, and galloped off so as not to lead the enemy directly to where the cavalry were collecting their forage and watering, and with great address, got to them unperceived by the enemy, calling out "draw your swords, Rangers, the rebels are coming." Capt. Shank, who was at Lee's farm waiting the return of the troops with their forage, in order to post them, immediately joined, and led them to the charge on the enemy's flank, which was somewhat exposed, while some of them were engaged in securing the horses at the back of Lee's farm; he broke them entirely.

Serjeant Wright dashed Major Macpherson, who commanded them, from his horse; but, leaving him in pursuit of others, that officer crept into a swamp, lay there unperceived during the action, and when it was over got off. Trumpeter

Barney dismounted and took a French officer, who commanded one of the divisions. The enemy's cavalry were so totally scattered, that they appeared no more; many of them were dismounted, and the whole would have been taken, had not a heavy fire out of the wood, from whence the highland company were now driven, protected them.

At this moment Lt. Col. Simcoe arrived; he had, at the first shot, ordered the infantry to march in column into the road towards the enemy, the light infantry company and Capt. Ewald's detachment excepted, which, being on the right, were moving straight to their own front to gain the wood. Collecting from the prisoners, that the enemy were in force, and that M. de la Fayette, and Generals Wayne and Steuben were at no great distance, the line was directed to be formed, spreading itself with wide intervals, and covering a great space of ground between the road on its left and Capt. Ewald on the right ; and, when formed, it was directed to advance to gain the wood, as it was his idea, to outflank the

enemy by the length of the line.

The principle which Lt. Colonel Simcoe always inculcated and acted on against the rifle-men, (whom he judged to be in the advanced corps of M. Fayette's army) was to rush upon them; when, if each separate company kept itself compact, there was little danger, even should it be surrounded, from troops who were without bayonets, and whose object it was to fire a single shot with effect: the position of an advancing soldier was calculated to lessen the true aim of the first shot, and his rapidity to prevent the rifleman, who requires some time to load, from giving a second; or at least to render his aim uncertain, and his fire by no means formidable. Lt. Col. Simcoe had withdrawn the cavalry from the fire of the enemy, and directed Captain Althouse, whose rifle company had been mounted, to dismount and to check them, if they sallied from the wood in pursuit of the cavalry, or for the purpose of reconnoitering and this he executed very effectively.

Capt. Branson had distinguished himself in the charge on the enemy's cavalry, and being dressed in red, he became a marked object to them : he was now ordered with the drivers and the cattle, to proceed to Williamsburg; messages were sent to Lord Cornwallis; and Lt. Allan, who acted as Quarter-Master, carried off the baggage that road, was directed to cut down trees, and to barricade the first place for the corps to rally, in case of necessity the fences were pulled down on the Jamestown road, in the rear of the cavalry, that the retreat might be made that way, if, which was every moment to be expelled, the enemy should have occupied the Williamsburg road in the rear.

Lt. Colonel Simcoe moved with the cavalry out of fight of the enemy, down the hill towards Jamestown road, and re-ascending at Lee's farm, there made a display of the whole force; then fell back again behind the hill, leaving only the front, a detachment of huzzars, both to prevent the left from being turned without notice, and to deceive the enemy into a belief that the whole cavalry (whose force they had already felt) were behind the eminences, waiting for an opportunity to fall upon their right flank; he returned rapidly with the rest of the cavalry undiscovered to the road, and formed them out of fight and out of reach of the enemy, partly in the road and partly on its left.

Beyond Capt. Ewald's flank there was open ground, which could easily be seen from the eminence on which Lt. Col. Simcoe was, and (by the turn of the Williamsburg road) the cavalry would have had quick access to it, had the enemy appeared there; by the position of the cavalry, it was also ready, in case the infantry had given way to flank the enemy, if they should issue form the wood in pursuit of it; the best substitute for want of the reserve, which, from the extent of the woods and the enemy's numbers, had been thrown into line.

Upon the left of the road the three pounder was placed, the amusette having broken down; there too the highland company had retired. The enemy now appeared in great force, lining the fences on the edge of the wood which separated it from the open ground in front of the infantry; and resting their right upon the open ground, by echelons; probably deceived by the appearance of the cavalry at Lee's farm; to add to their reasons for not advancing, one cannon shot, and no more, was ordered to be fired at the body, which appeared to be at the greatest distance. The infantry was now in line, but with intervals between the companies, advancing as fast as the ploughed fields they had to cross would

admit. Lt. Col. Simcoe did not expect victory, but he was determined to try for it just as his best hopes were to obtain and line the wood, checking the enemy's advance, 'till such times as the convoy was in security, and then to retreat.

He had the most general and particular confidence in the officers and soldiers of his corps, who were disciplined enthusiasts in the cause of their country , and who, having been ever victorious, thought it impossible to suffer defeat, nor had he less reliance on the acknowledged military talents of his friend Ewald, and the cool and tried courage of his jaegers; the event fully justified the expression which he used in the beginning of the action, "I will take care of the left; while Ewald lives, the right flank will never be turned."

Fortune now decided in favour of the British troops; the road from Norwal's mills was enclosed with high and strong fences, a considerable body of the enemy being on the right of the road, and, seeing the infantry advancing, faced and were crossing these fences to flank them : they did not observe the cavalry, which, while they were in this disorder, left not the moment; but, led by Capt. Shank, charged them up the road, and upon its left, entirely broke and totally dispersed them. The infantry were ordered to advance, and they rushed on with the greatest rapidity, the enemy's fire was in vain, they were driven from the fences and the wood.

Capt. Ewald turned their left flank, and gave them a severe fire as they fled in the utmost confusion; could he have been supported, as he wished, by a very small body of fresh bayonet men, such was the advantage of the ground, that the enemy, in confusion, and panic stricken, would have received a very severe blow, before it could have been possible for them to rally.

Cornet Jones, who led the first division of cavalry, was unfortunately killed; he was an active, sensible, promising officer. The mounted riflemen of the Queen's Rangers charged with Capt. Shank; the gallant Serjeant McPherson, who led them, was mortally wounded. Two of the men of this detachment were carried away by their impetuosity so far as to pass beyond the enemy, and their horses were killed: they, however, secreted themselves in the wood under some fallen logs, and, when the enemy fled from that spot, they returned in safety to the corps.

By a mistake, scarcely avoidable in the tumult of action, Capt. Shank was not supported, as was intended, by the whole of his cavalry, by which fewer prisoners were taken than might have been; that valuable officer was in the most imminent danger, in fighting his way back through the enemy, who fired upon him, and wounded the Trumpeter Barney and killed some of the huzzars, who attended him.

The grenadier company, commanded by Capt. McGill, signalized by their gallantry as well as by their dress, lost several valuable men.

Capt. Stevenson was distinguished as usual; his chosen and well-trained light infantry were obstinately opposed; but they carried their point with the loss of a fourth of their numbers, killed and wounded.

An affair of this nature necessarily afforded a great variety of gallant actions in individuals. Capt. McRae reported to Lt. Col. Simcoe, that his subaltern, Lt. Charles Dunlop, who had served in the Queen's Rangers from thirteen years of age, led on his division on horseback, without suffering a man to fire, watching the enemy, and giving a signal to his men to lay down whenever a party of their's was about to fire; he arrived at the fence where the enemy had been posted with his arms loaded, a conduct that might have been decisive of the action; fortunately he escaped unhurt.

The whole of the loss of the Queen's Rangers amounted to ten killed, and twenty-three wounded; among the latter was Lt. Swift Armstrong, and Ensign Jarvis, acting with the grenadiers; the jaegers had two or three men wounded and one killed. It may be supposed, in the course of so long a service, there was scarcely a man of them, whose death did not call forth a variety of situations, in which his courage had been distinguished, or his value exemplified; and it seemed to everyone, as if the flower of the regiment had been cut off.

As the whole series of the service of light troops gives the greatest latitude for the exertion of individual talents, and of individual courage, so did the present situation require the most perfect combination of them.

Every division, every officer, every soldier had his share in the merit of the action; mistake in the one might have brought on cowardice in the other, and a single panic stricken soldier would probably have infected a platoon, and led to the utmost confusion and ruin; so that Lt. Col. Simcoe has ever considered this action as the climax of a campaign of five years, as the result of true discipline acquired in that space by unremitted diligence, toil, and danger, as an honourable victory earned by veteran intrepidity.

The instant Lt. Col. Simcoe could draw off and collect his force, and had communicated with Capt. Ewald, it was thought proper to retreat; the information obtained from two and thirty prisoners, many of them officers and of different corps, making it expedient to do; the wounded men were collected into Spencer's ordinary, there being no wagons with the detachment, and they were left there with the surgeon's mate, and a flag of truce. The infantry filed off to the right, and the cavalry closed the rear; the party soon arrived at a brook, on the opposite and commanding side of which Lt. Allen, with the pioneers, had cut down some trees, and was proceeding to give it such defences as it was capable of receiving.

In less than two miles, Lt. Col. Simcoe met Earl Cornwallis, and the advance of his army, and returned with them towards Spencer's ordinary; he reported to his Lordship, what he had learnt from an examination of the rebel prisoners, and by his own and his officers observations; that the enemy were, at the least, twelve hundred strong in action, above three times the numbers of his corps; that Fayette's army was at no great distance; that they had marched twenty-eight miles, and had no provisions. Lt. Colonel Simcoe added, that he had effectively destroyed the Diescung bridge.

Earl Cornwallis examined the prisoners, and observed to Lt. Col. Simcoe, that it was a march of great hazard in Fayette, as on the least previous intimation he must have been cut off. On the approach to Spencer's, Lt. Col. Simcoe galloped forward, and was very happy to find, that his wounded men were not prisoners, none of the enemy having approached them. and he found a foraging party of Earl Cornwallis's army, with the wagons on which the wounded and the dead were placed. So little idea w-as there entertained of Fayette's move, that this foraging party had proceeded some miles on the Williamsburg road, and would have been certainly taken, had it not been for the action at Spencer's. It is reported, and not without probability, that a patrol of the enemy met with this party on the road, where it was natural to expect Lord Cornwallis's army, and took it for his advance guard, and that this belief prevented them from renewing the attack.

Lt. Col. Tarleton soon after arrived at Spencer's; he had advanced up the Willlamsburg road, and in the wood in front of Spencer's, met with a great number of arms, thrown away, and other symptoms of the confusion in which the enemy had fled; the army returned to Williamsburg, and the Queen's Rangers were hutted on the right at Queen's creek.

At the commencement of the action, the bat-men and their horses, feeding at Lee's farm, were taken; they were all rescued, Lt. Col. Simcoe's groom excepted, the only prisoner the enemy carried off. It was generally reported, that the person who had been sent to Fayette's camp, from Cooper's mills, conducted Gen. Wayne thither, about four o'clock in the morning, who, with a large force, charged with fixed bayonets, the fires which the Queen's Rangers had but just quitted. M. Fayette, in his public letters, stated the loss of the British at one hundred and fifty killed and wounded, and attributed it to the skill of his rifle-men; his own he diminished, recapitulating that only of the continental troops, and taking no notice of the militia; it is certain they had a great many killed and wounded, exclusive of the prisoners. The rifle-men, however dextrous in the use of their arms, were by no means the most formidable of the rebel troops; not being armed with bayonets, they permitted their opponents to take liberties with them which otherwise would have been highly improper.

Cornet Jones was buried at Willlamsburg the next day, with military honours. It was given out in the public orders, at Willlamsburg, on the 28th of June, that: "Lord Cornwallis desires Lt.

Col. Simcoe will accept of his warmest acknowledgments for his spirited and judicious conduct in the action of the 26th instant, when he repulsed and defeated so superior a force of the enemy. He likewise desires that Lt. Col. Simcoe will communicate his thanks to the officers and soldiers of the Queen's Rangers, and to Capt. Ewald and the detachment of jaegers."

Corporal Jacob Smith

Jacob Smith enlisted in the Queen's Rangers in 1777, serving with them until the end of the Revolutionary War. He was resettled in Nova Scotia in 1783, but in 1785 returned to his family farm Delaware County, Pennsylvania.

When I left my father and mother, I was in my twenty-first year of my age, and then my troubles just began. The reason of my travelling was because I could not be traitor to my King, now I bid farewell to all my playmates for a while.

9th November, 1777

I left Brandywine Hundred and all my friends and relations and arrived on board the Stanley Brigantine of 12 guns, Richard, Whitworth Master, and he gave me the best usage that the vessel could afford. I dined at the table with himself and we had punch in the afternoon, and you may be sure a raw country lad like me thought it fines times; but stop a little.

19th November

At night the enemy evacuated Mud Island Fort.

20th November

His Majesty's army took possession of said fort, finding legs, arms and pieces of dead bodies blown about the fort.

23rd November

I left the brig and got on board a ship bound to Philadelphia. But now my trouble begins. When I came to Philadelphia, I saw no one I knew, the patrols marching up and down the streets, apprehending everyone that could not give a straight account of their business. I began to think I was in a fine box for a change. I found no punch there for me.

24th November

For a change I enlisted to serve his Majesty in the Queen's Rangers as a private soldier two years and I was to receive a £5 bounty etc. I joined one Captain Smith's company, but being middling tall and straight, I was eyed by the captain of the Grand Company, and he gave me no rest until I was moved.

1st December

The Army marched to Chestnut Hill above Germantown and burned several houses and destroyed some of the enemy's property.

4th December

Army marched back to Germantown and proceeded from there to White Marsh and had a skirmish with the enemy. I thought I had brought myself in a fine scrape. I stood sentry this night where I heard the enemy talking very plain.

5th December

Army marched back to Philadelphia and burned the Rising Sun tavern between Germantown and Philadelphia, you must think I was glad when I got back safe to my former quarters again.

24th December

I was drafted into the Grenadier Company, commanded by Captain Richard

Armstrong. Our Regiment went out once or twice every week to cover the country people coming to Philadelphia market.

26th February, 1778

Our Regiment and the 42nd cross the Delaware River at Cooper's Ferry`and marched to Hattenfield for forage.

3rd March

Back to Cooper's Ferry.

4th March

The enemy came down under command of Wayne and drove in our guards and charged our lines, but was forced to retreat after having his horse shot under him.

13th April

Our Regiment and the Light Infantry of the line marched to Chestnut Hill to cover some refugees with a drove of cattle taken from the enemy drovers and returned the same day to Philadelphia with upwards of 80 fat bullocks.

7th July

Sailed from Sandy Hook to New York.

28th August

Made Corporal in Captain McGill's Company.

11th March, 1780

I was ordered to be assistant in the Regimental store under Sergeant Robert Gardner.

18th April

The fleet arrived at Stona Bay, South Carolina.

12th May

The garrison of Charlestown marched out into the commons, grounded their arms, the British marched in and took possession, the prisoners after grounding their arms marched back into the town.

30th August, 1781

The French fleet under the command of the Count De Grasses blocked up York River with 27 sails of the line, they took the loyalist 20-gun ship.

2nd September

Four French ships came up in the York River and anchored about 5 or 6 miles from the town.

5th September

Early this morning Lord Cornwallis with the principal part of the army marched from York towards Williamsburg in order to bring the combined armies to battle.

22nd September

Between 1 and 2 o'clock this morning five fire ships were sent down the river with the tide to set the French shipping afire, but to no effect, the French ships slipped their cable and went out of the river.

30th September

We have account that Admiral Digby is arrived at New York with 10 sail of the Line and the King's third son in the fleet; this morning the left wing of the combined army made an attempt to storm a redoubt of ours laying on the York side of the river, our people received their fire till they began to pull away the abatis, then gave them a general fire with cannon and small arms, until the enemy were obliged to retreat after leaving 100 men dead and 50 wounded on the ground. In another part our people quit their out works to draw the enemy, in which they took the advantage of and our men immediately charged the works and the enemy as quickly retreated from them in this they lost Colonel Miland and the commanding officer of another detachment.

The French troops draw three quarters of a pound of flour and a half a pound of beef per day, the American draw Indian meal; our batteries keep a constant cannonading day and night.

3rd October

Last evening the Legion, Mounted Infantry, and part of the Queen's Rangers went into the country for forage, came across French Cavalry, charged them 3 times, but were beaten off with spears, had an officer killed and 3 or 4 men wounded. We hear that the enemy's combined army consists of upwards of 40,000 effective men fit for Action.

10th October

This morning there was a party of the Queen's Rangers went on board a boat up the York River, but returned without landing. The battery keeps constant cannonading on both sides.

11th October

The French Batteries set the Charon 5th gun ship and three transports on fire with hot shot; they keep constant cannonading on both sides. This evening the enemy attempted to storm a redoubt on the bank of York River, but was beat back to their works.

12th October

Continue the siege on both sides with great bravery.

13th October

This afternoon the enemy slacked firing, it is they fire faster than they can get supplies.

14th October

This evening the enemy stormed our two redoubts on the left flank; such firing never was heard in America, you would have thought Heaven and Earth were coming together.

15th October

Our army seems in poor spirits, this day continual cannonading on both sides.

16th October

This morning at daybreak Colonel Abercrombey with the British Light Infantry stormed and took the enemy's principal redoubt, spiked up eleven pieces of their cannon.

17th October

A cessation of arms commenced between the armies.

19th October

The regiment ordered to parade at 6 o'clock in the morning with knapsacks and accoutrement. The garrison marched out at 5 o'clock in the afternoon and delivered up their arms and accoutrements to the French and American troops, then returned to their encampment. The French grenadiers marched in and took possession of the redoubts on the right and the Americans on the left of the garrison.

27th December, 1781

I received 5 days beef for the regiment but no flour or meal. The regiment marched from Virginia and encamped at Lancaster, Pennsylvania over winter.

1st July, 1782

I drew 4 days provisions for the regiment also two months soap and candles.

4th July

Sergeant Kelly of the American Artillery by being so much in a hurry a showing his great capabilities in firing the laminations of joy got blown off his feet with the sponge and badly wounded.

28th July

Sergeant Kelly was buried in the English Church yard.

21st September, 1783

Regiment set sail from New York for Nova Scotia.

24th September

The ship caught fire and caused quite a commotion for a while, but they succeeded in getting it out, with very little damage to the ship.

18th December, 1785

I got home to my father's after being away 8 years, one month and nine days.

Captain J.F.D. Smyth

John Ferdinand Dalziel Smyth joined the Queen's Rangers after escaping from imprisonment by rebels in 1777. He served throughout the war as a company commander. In his civilian life he was a doctor and gentleman farmer, with properties in Maryland, Pennsylvania and Western Florida. His diary below chronicles his escape from jail in Baltimore.

On the 30th December at night, 1775, I watched the moment the two sentinels fell asleep on their posts at the door, and unscrewing the lock, made my escape, with letters, and every necessary order, but was obliged to leave all my clothes. There was a deep encrusted snow, and most dreadful roads, so that my journey was beyond expression fatiguing, especially as I left my horse, and went on foot, to prevent any suspicion of my route; as no one could imagine, that a journey over the Alegany mountains to Mississippi and Detroit, would be attempted at that season of the year, by any person alone and on foot. To pass along with more privacy, I endeavoured to go up on the other side of Potomack river, but in attempting to cross on the of ice, broke in and almost got lost; it was snowing and freezing at the same time, and I had seven miles over the mountains to go, before I came to a house to warm myself. At last, when I reached it, there was no fire, and I could not stay, so I travelled in that wet and frozen condition all day, and at night lay before the fire, at the house of a poor ignorant Dutchman.

On the 1st January, 1776, I reached the mouth of Connicochege at sunrise. It was frozen half over, I broke the ice, stripped and waded it through, up to my breast, and, hearing of a pursuit, struck off the road into the north mountain, travelled all day through fatiguing and encrusted snow, and stayed during the night (for I slept not) under a rock in the mountain.

Jan. 2d, travelled all day in the mountain, and at night scraped away the snow by the side of a tree, made a fire, and slept a little. On the 3d January directed my course towards the road again, being then behind the pursuit, and stayed all night at a miserable house by the fire, I passed by the name of Brescoe. Here I heard a thousand falsehoods told about me, and was obliged to join in the abuse against myself; they all said, that we ought immediately to have been put to death when taken.

On the 4th Jan. I had three violent falls on the ice, by which I received a bad strain in one ankle, and a deep wound in my opposite foot; this rendered traveling excessively painful. However, with me there was no alternative but death to stop, or life to proceed; and in this distressing manner I continued to push on, until the 12th of January, when after wading numbers of creeks and rivers, and getting over the Alegany mountains, I was retaken on the Yohiogeny, close by the Ohio, by a party of nine ruffians returning from Pittsburg in pursuit of me. They set me on a pack horse, on a wooden pack saddle, tied my arms behind me, and my legs under the horse's belly, took off the bridle, and put a great bell on the horse, and in that manner they drove the horse and me before them, over slippery ways covered with ice, and over all the dreadful precipices of the Alegany and Blue mountains, for the first day and night, and for the next three days; every night lying on the bare ground. Travelling in this violent rapid manner, as I am informed since, saved me, as a Captain and thirty men from near Pittsburg, pursued us, under oath to kill me, then they heard I was retaken, and after riding after us a day and a half, despairing to overtake us, they returned. During all this time I tasted different nothing but water, and had but one meal of indifferent food, which probably in some degree contributed also to my recovery, by abating the inflammation of the wound in my foot, and the strain in my ankle, both of which were prodigiously swelled, and so violently painful, that for my life I could not walk a hundred yards, and entirely deprived me of sleep.

I was then delivered up again to the Committee of Hagar's Town, who made use of every artifice of promises and threats to corrupt my principles, and when all would not avail, ordered me to be carried to the Congress to Philadelphia, in irons. A fresh guard, with a Major, a Captain, two Lieutenants, &c. then set off with me, tied as before, and my horse tied also with two ropes, and led by two of the guard, accompanied with drum and fife, beating the rogue's march, which they seemed particularly fond of. Fifteen miles from Frederick Town, a Captain and fifty rebels came to take me from my guard, to carry me back to Frederick Town, to two hundred more, who had assembled, and were waiting there to murder me at once, in order as they said, to save the country expense. It required no small address to persuade this rabble out of their intentions, as they were sent by the rest on purpose, but at last they suffered us to proceed. They carried me through Crissop's Town, Hancock's Town, Little Town, McAllastar's Town, York, and Lancaster; in each of the last places I was lodged in gaol; and at last arrived at Philadelphia, dragged all this way, being several hundred miles, like a criminal or felon going to execution.

The Congress, to express their approbation of the cruelty and zeal of those who retook me, gave each of them a commission, and fifteen pounds to bear each of their expenses, and to the principal, seventy-five dollars extraordinary, and a captain's commission of riflemen, as a reward. By the Congress I was sent to the Council of Safety (properly of destruction) and by them to the common gaol, where a very large pair of irons were brought for me, but a gentleman present went out and got an order against it.

I was then thrown into a room in the criminal apartment, the door constantly locked, no person, even in the gaol, allowed to speak to me, in a cold vaulted room, without bed, blanket, or straw, chair or table, obliged to lie on the bare floor, with a log of wood under my head, in the middle of a severe winter, and sometimes three days without a drop of water or any kind of drink. In this condition I remained for three weeks, and without changing my shirt, or having my clothes off for thirty-three days; also, very sick, and very lame. To think on all I suffered, one would imagine that human nature could hardly support it; but a man can at sometimes undergo much more than would at other times destroy him.

Imagining that they intended in that manner to take away my life, I wrote with a pencil on a card (nothing else being allowed me) desiring they would order me to immediate execution, and not destroy me by inches. They then had me brought before them, and behaved very politely to me, making apologies for what was past, and promising better in future, but declared their astonishment at my desperate attempt, as they called it, of reaching Detroit or Illinois, alone, and on foot, at that season of the year, through a hostile country, and without money (as I had only the guinea the Committee had left me). But although they promised to render my confinement more supportable, yet I was ordered back to gaol, almost in the same situation as before. I take this opportunity to acknowledge many obligations to Captain Duncan Campbell, of the Royal Emigrants, who was at that time also a close prisoner, and did me every service in his power, that my precluded situation would admit of. Captain Campbell about this time was so ill that he was in great danger of death, having been in gaol four months, and at last only to save his life, they admitted him to parole. I was then removed into his room in the front, with Mr. Kirkland; and Major General Prescot was put into the room in the criminal apartment I was taken out of, where he was kept until the dampness of the walls, and the unwholesomeness of the place, caused his wounds to break out afresh; then he was removed.

After some days, the gaoler brought me a paper containing a dirty scandalous parole, which he said, was sent to me to sign, as they wanted to atone now for my former ill usage. One Mr. Nixon had interested himself to procure it; but as Lieutenant-Colonel Connolly and Lieutenant Cameron were not offered their paroles also, I refused to sign it, and was then put into the room along with them. In two days after, Lieutenant Colonel Connolly got the liberty of the gaol at large and another room, but they nailed down the windows on Lieutenant Cameron and me, and chained the door, so as not to admit a breath of fresh air to us, debarred the. use of pen and ink, no person whatever allowed to see or speak to us, and totally precluded from the whole world, as effectually as if we had been in our graves; in this manner were we kept for six months, of, which was represented until our lives were despaired to the Congress, by Dr. B. Rush, Dr. Cadwalader, and Dr. Bond, in written memorials. That distrustful junto ordered a committee of themselves, composed of a Mr. Wilcot, and a Thomas McKean of Newcastle, to come to us, and see our situation and state of health Mr. Wilcot talked like a moderate man, but the violent raging rebel McKean, introduced himself by abusing, in the grossest terms, The King, Parliament, and Ministry; the whole army and navy; and particularly Lord Dunmore and General Prescot. He told us, for our comfort, that we should be retained for retaliation; that if Allen, or Proctor, or any of their leaders were executed, we should share the same fate; said we ought to think ourselves happy, not to be in irons, as their prisoners were always kept in irons by the British. In order to preserve us for that purpose, he ordered our windows to be opened; after some time, an order came from Congress permitting us to walk two hours every day, with two sentinels, in a hot, nasty, suffocating yard of the gaol. But this was allowed us only for a few days. All this time the gaoler charged us four dollars a week each, for our diet only, though very indifferent, and twenty shillings a week for fire and candle. The Congress allowed us only two dollars weekly each, so that this infamous villain the gaoler, extorted every farthing of money from us, as far as our credit then would go. But being determined not to run in debt, I refused to pay them any more than the Congress allowed, and was obliged to subsist five weeks upon bread and water alone. The gaoler 's name was Thomas Dewees, as tyrannical, cruel, infamous a villain as ever existed. Sometime before this Major MacDonald, and twenty-five prisoners from Carolina were brought to gaol, forced to march all the way from Carolina on foot. They were confined in these close rooms for six weeks, and were then allowed the liberty of the gaol only every third day. The Congress in July, put in two new gaolers of the name Jewell, if possible more cruel and tyrannical than the former, and ordered the old gaoler, and all the debtors and criminals to another prison; and kept only what they called prisoners of state in ours. The cruelties practised there are almost incredible, and at least equal to the Spanish inquisition prison. The gaol was constantly guarded by one sentinel on each side without, two in the front, two in the yard, three in the passage below, and three within the passage above, and the guard room in the prison. The restrictions on us were so severe, that we were not allowed to speak to any in different rooms.

Sept. 20th, Jewell accused me of speaking to Colonel Connolly, and ordered a Serjeant and nine men to carry me into a nasty guard room, then into a damp cold empty room, where I was obliged to lie on the bare floor, and that gave me a violent cholic. I was extremely ill, without any care or notice taken of me, and lay in that sick helpless condition, locked up in a room by myself, without the least assistance whatsoever. Soon after that I was seized with a dysentery, which continued on me seven weeks, and reduced me to the point of death, yet still I was locked up without any care, attendance, or notice. Dr. Benjamin Rush, one of the Congress, a man eminent in Physic, but as eminent in rebellion and still more so in deceit, after tantalizing me with hopes of a parole, exchange, and professions of very great regard and commiseration, one day informed me, that many members of Congress said they personally knew me to be so determinedly inimical to the American States, and that I had always used such interest and influence against them, that I need not expect any kind of indulgence whatsoever, not even to save life.

Thanks to Heaven I recovered; then Lieutenant Cameron, Lieutenant McLean, and myself, were put in a room together, selected from the rest, to experience the dire effects of their inhuman malice, and a sentinel placed at our door to prevent our speaking or being spoken to. In December, the gaoler came with a guard, and plundered us again, under pretence of searching for papers, and abused us in the most injurious manner.

December 10th, the Carolina prisoners were sent off to Baltimore under a guard, and on the 11th, sixty Jersey men from were sent away tied with ropes to each other, under small guard. Our confinement was now become so unsupportable, that even death would have been an agreeable deliverance. This set us on a desperate scheme of breaking through; and with an incredible difficulty and labour we got through the vaulting, cut afterward with a pen-knife through a two-inch plank, and got up, by the cupola, on the top of the house, intending to descend on a rope, to cross the Delaware, and push for the British army then at Burlington, only miles off. But our rope, consisting of sheets, blankets, &c. gave way with Cameron, who descended first; and he fell forty-eight feet perpendicular on the pavement. His life was miraculously saved, but his bones were broke; and he has suffered amazingly ever since.

McLean and I were then stripped of our money, papers, and every individual thing we had, even my journal, and were thrown into the dungeon for condemned felons, without light, or bedclothes, or even our great coats to preserve us from the intense cold; and without food or drink for twenty-four hours. Here I expected nothing but to end my days in misery, but the goodness and justice of our cause supported my spirits, and I felt nothing for myself; all my distress was for poor Cameron, as they all cried, "let him die and be damned," and wished me the same condition. In this situation they kept us until orders were given for our removal to Baltimore, as they every day expected an attack on Philadelphia. They then brought out twenty of us in all, viz. seven gentlemen, eight privates belonging to the twenty-third and other regiments, and five sailors; put us in irons, every two ironed together, and with a guard of fifty or sixty chosen Dutchmen, marched us on foot to Baltimore, and that night lodged us in Chester gaol, without taking off our irons at all. The irons kept me from sleep every night, besides they were too small, causing me to swell prodigiously, and were very painful. Yet in this condition they marched us until ten o'clock every night, which was particularly severe on me, who had covered with blisters. At the head of Elk, at the head of Chesapeak Bay, we were put on board of one privateer, and our baggage on board of another. There were two rebel Colonels, one Price, a hatter, and Gunby, formerly a skipper of a bay craft, that maltreated and insulted us very much. They took possession of the cabin, &c. and we were thrown indiscriminately into the hold, without any thing to lie on but pig iron and stones, and no kind of covering. The snow was falling fast upon us, and they would not suffer the hatches to be shut to keep it off. In this condition we were kept for two days and nights, every two chained together; under a guard of sixty awkward Dutchmen, besides the privateer's crew, until we arrived at Baltimore, having but one very indifferent meal of food, that too we brought with us, and through the whole journey we were obliged to bear our own expenses.

The skippers (or if you please to call them captains) of these privateers were most notoriously insulting and rebellious, their names Patterson and Robinson. At Baltimore we were much better used, only the two Messrs. Goodriches were selected from us and thrown into the gaol. We were kept under guard. The Maryland matrosses mounted guard on us for two days, then the Baltimore militia for the two days more, but they were so very friendly to us, that the Congress ordered them away, and obliged the artillery to do constant duty. There were a hundred and ten of them, and fifty-two composed our guard. They were almost all Europeans, and generally friendly, so that could I have brought them clear off, the greatest part would have come away with me. There were seven always on duty on us. Four of us escaped into an adjoining room, and from the window of it we descended by a small rope, which cut my hands very much, by slipping through them. I had provided a sloop, seven miles below the fort and chain, and by the assistance of a guide got on board, and by next night we were in Hooper's Streights, above a hundred miles, after being much alarmed by a little privateer that kept about us. I landed first, and soon found friends from whom we met with a most cordial protection, as they offered me two hundred men to guard us to Lewes Town, about sixty miles. But we chose to travel in the night with only two, whose names I must now conceal, as they are yet in the power of the rebels. This was the 11th January, 1777.

At the mouth of Delaware we expected to find the Roebuck, but she sailed from there the 8th, and from that time no ship of war had touched at that important station, until the 12th March, except the Falcon, which landed some prisoners, and burnt a schooner at the mouth of Indian river, on the 20th January. Capt. Linzee of the Falcon, though he landed some prisoners near the place where we were, could not be prevailed on to wait, only two hours for us, although he was earnestly intreated to do so by Mr. Slater, who got on board his barge in a punt that could carry but two persons, and he was by him particularly informed that we were British prisoners, escaped from a long and most cruel confinement, and that two of the first gentleman of property and interest in the country were with us, wanting much to get on board, being driven from their homes to avoid the persecution of the rebels. This was exceedingly discouraging to all the friends to government, and one of the most truly mortifying to us we ever met with; next morning we viewed the ocean with many a longing earnest look, still flattering ourselves with hope that the ship might return, but all in vain.

I continued with the two gentlemen I have just mentioned, T. Robinson and B. Manlove, Esqrs., well-armed, and we all kept concealed, until another ship of war should arrive on the coast. During this time the rebel frigate Randolph of 36 guns, came down from Philadelphia, proudly cruised off and on the Cape for three days, then stood out to sea. Taking her for a king's ship, we had almost gone on board, but soon were undeceived by our friends, who were indefatigable in assisting us.

During our concealment an insurrection of the loyalists happened in Somerset and Worster counties, concerning some assistance afforded us in escaping. Eleven hundred loyalists had assembled; but as there was no prospect of any support, I took the greatest pains to persuade them to disperse peaceably, and at length effected it, which at that time saved them from utter ruin. Apprehensive of being discovered, and despairing of a man of war arriving on the coast, we were forming many schemes of proceeding to New York; sometimes of crossing the bay and travelling by land, sometimes of rowing in a canoe all along the coast, and many more equally hazardous and enterprising.

At last, on the 12th March, we saw two ships of war and a sloop standing towards the Cape, and at night eleven of us set out in a pettiauger, with oars, from Rehoboth bay; we had six miles to row to get out of the inlet over the bar, and afterwards eighteen miles out at sea, to reach the place where we expected the ships would anchor. The night was very dark, stormy, and blustering, with much thunder, lightning, wind and rain; having rowed above eighteen miles, a violent squall right a head obliged us to turn back, but we could not get on shore for the breakers, which ran prodigiously high.

The night was so dark we could not possibly find the channel over the bar of the inlet, without being all dashed to pieces; so, we went about once more, and stood again for the cape. Having rowed backwards, and forward to no purpose the greater part of the night, in search of a ship, a perfect storm forced us to purpose the greater part of the night, and, as it happened to be close by a rebel guard, we were obliged to remain without fire, noise or motion on the open beach, in the rain and snow, which was then deep, until daybreak, when we set out again, and after rowing about for a long time in a prodigious thick fog, we heard a cock crow, and thereby found the Preston, in such a mist that the ship was not visible twenty yards. My joy was inexpressible on seeing the name Preston on her stern, being in some apprehensions of rebel frigates. I never parted with my arms until I got on board, then I sent them all back. The worthy Commodore Hotham, and all the officers on board received us in the most kind and friendly manner so that it almost effaced the remembrance of our disappointment from the Falcon.

We had not been half an hour on board, when the most violent hurricane from the land came on that ever I saw; it was so sudden and so violent, that before our canoe could be got on board, it tore the iron bolt from her head, drove her away, and filled her in an instant; it also drove the Preston out to sea; and every officer on board repeatedly congratulated us on our most fortunate escape; because had we not found the ship, (which was astonishing in such a fog) we must every man have inevitably perished, as she was four or five leagues league from land, and we could not have got one league farther before the storm came on.

Very fortunately we immediately got a passage to New York in the Daphne, which convoyed four fine prizes safe into port on the 19th March, and shall never forget the particular obligations I am under to the worthy Capt. Chinery, and every one of the officers of the Daphne, for their truly kind, hospitable and friendly treatment, during the whole time since we were on board.

I have omitted a thousand instances of the most mortifying cruelty and insult I continually met with, during near eighteen months captivity, and have only related plain

matters of fact, without the least heightening or embellishment, the truth of all which can be vouched for by numbers of the best authority and credit, as well as by:

J. F. D. Smyth, Captain, Queen's Rangers.
New-York, Dec 25., 1777.

The War of 1812

To some historians no more than a side note to the Napoleonic Wars raging in Europe, the conflict was an existential one for the British colonies in North America. Canadian myth-making has embraced the story of British soldiers, Canadian militia and Indigenous warriors fighting side by side to protect the nascent nation. While certainly overblown, all three of these groups had interests to defend in Canada, and they did so successfully against American opportunistic aggression. The 1st and 3rd Regiments of York Militia, perpetuated by the modern day Regiment, played a significant role throughout the war.

Lieutenant George Ridout

George Ridout was the second son of the Surveyor General of Upper Canada and a member of one of the colony's most prominent families. He served as a Lieutenant in the Grenadier Company of the Third Regiment, York Militia during the War of 1812. He was captured by American Forces during the Battle of York.

Brown's Point, October 14th, 1812.

About half an hour before daylight yesterday morning, Tuesday, the 13th October, being stationed at one of the batteries between Fort George and Queenston, I heard a heavy cannonading from Fort Grey, situate on the height of the Mountain, on the American side, and commanding the town of Queenston.

The lines had been watched with all the care and attention which the extent of our force rendered possible, and such was the fatigue which our men under- went from want of rest and exposure to the inclement weather which had just preceded, that they welcomed with joy the prospect of a field which they thought would be decisive. Their spirits were high, and their confidence in the General unbounded.

From our battery at Brown's Point, about two miles from Queenston, we had the whole scene most completely in our view.

Day was just glimmering.

The cannon from both sides of the river roared incessantly.

Queenston was illuminated by the continual discharge of small arms. This last circumstance convinced us that some of the enemy had landed, and in a few moments, as the day advanced and objects became more visible, we saw a number of Americans in boats attempting to land upon our shore, amidst a tremendous shower of shot of all description, which was skillfully and incessantly levelled at them.

No orders had been given to Captain Cameron, who commanded our detachment of York Militia, what conduct to pursue in case of an attack at Queenston; and as it had been suggested to him that in the event of a landing being attempted there, the enemy would probably endeavour, by various attacks, to distract our force, he hesitated at first as to the propriety of withdrawing his men from the station assigned them to defend.

He soon saw, however, that every exertion was required in aid of the troops engaged above us, and without further delay, marched us to the scene of action. On our road. General Brock passed us. He had galloped from Niagara, unaccompanied by his aide-de-camp, or a single attendant.

He waved his hand to us, desired us to follow with expedition, and proceeded with all speed to the Mountain. Lieutenant-Colonel McDonell and Captain Glegg passed immediately after. At the time the enemy began to cross, there were but two companies of the 49th regiment, the Grenadiers and the Light Company, and I believe three small companies of militia, to oppose them.

Their reception was such as did honour to the courage and management of our troops.

The grape shot and musket balls poured upon them at close quarters, as they approached the shore, and made incredible havoc.

A single discharge of grape from a brass six-pounder, directed by Captain Dennis, of the 49th Grenadiers, destroyed fifteen in a boat.

Three of the bateaux landed at the hollow below Mr. Hamilton's garden, in Queenston, and were met by a party of militia and a few regulars, who slaughtered almost the whole of them, taking the rest prisoners.

Several other boats were so shattered and disabled that the men in them threw down their arms and came on shore, merely to deliver themselves up prisoners of war.

Thus far things had proceeded successfully, and the General on his approach to the Mountain was greeted with the intelligence that all our villainous aggressors were destroyed or taken.

As we advanced with our company we met troops of Americans on their way to Fort George, under guard, and the road was lined with miserable wretches suffering under wounds of all descriptions, and crawling to our houses for protection and comfort. The spectacle struck us, who were unused to such scenes, with horror; but we hurried to the Mountain, impressed with the idea that the enemy's attempt was already frustrated, and the business of the day nearly completed.

Another brigade of four boats was just

then crossing, and the 49th Light Company, who had been stationed on the Mountain, were ordered down to assist in preventing their landing. No sooner had they descended than the enemy appeared in force above them. They had probably landed before the rest, while it was yet dark, and remained concealed by the rough crags of the Mountain.

They possessed themselves of our battery on the height.

General Brock rushed up the Mountain on foot, with some troops, to dislodge them, but they were so advantageously posted and kept up so tremendous a fire that the small number ascending were driven back.

The General then rallied, and was proceeding up the right of the Mountain to attack them in flank, when he received a ball in his breast. Several of the 49th assembled round him. One poor fellow was severely wounded by a cannon ball and fell across the General. They succeeded, however, in conveying his body to Queenston. We were halted a few moments in Mr. Hamilton's garden, where we were exposed to the shot from the American battery at Fort Grey, and from several field-pieces directly opposite to us, besides an incessant and disorderly fire of musketry from the sides of the Mountain.

In a few minutes, we were ordered to advance on the Mountain. The nature of the ground and the galling fire prevented any kind of order in ascending. We soon scrambled to the top, at the right of the battery, which they had gained, and were in some measure covered by the woods. There we stood and gathered the men as they advanced, and formed them in a line.

The fire was too hot to admit of delay. Scarcely more than fifty collected, about thirty of whom were of our company, headed by Captain Cameron, and the remainder of the 49th Light Company, commanded by Captain Williams.

Lieutenant-Colonel McDonell was there mounted, and animating the men to charge. He was seconded with great spirit and valour by Captain Williams, who exclaimed, "Feel firmly to the right, my lads, advance steadily, charge them home, and they cannot stand you."

But the attempt was unsuccessful.

The enemy were just in front covered by bushes and logs. They were in no kind of order, and were three or four hundred in number. They perceived us forming, and, at about thirty yards distance, fired. Lieutenant-Colonel McDonell who was on the left our party, most heroically calling upon us to advance, received a shot in his body and fell. His horse was at the same instant killed.

Captain Williams, who was at the other extremity of our little band, fell the next moment apparently dead.

The remainder of our men advanced a few paces, discharged their pieces, and retired down the Mountain.

Lieutenant McLean was wounded in the thigh, and Captain Cameron, in his attempt to save Colonel McDonell, exposed himself to a shower of musketry, which he most miraculously escaped.

He succeeded in bearing off his friend, and Captain Williams recovered from the momentary effect of the wound in his head, in time to escape down the mountain. This happened, I think, about 10a.m.

Our forces rallied about a mile below.

General Sheaffe, with the 41st from Fort George, nearly three hundred in number, came up soon after with the field-pieces of the Car Brigade.

All the force that could be collected was now mustered, and marched through the fields back of Queenston, ascended the Mountain on the right, and remained in the woods in rear of the enemy till intelligence was gained of their position. During this time, the Americans were landing fresh troops unmolested, and carrying back their dead and wounded in their return boats.

About three o'clock p.m. General Sheaffe advanced through the woods, towards the battery on the Mountain, with the main body, composed of the 41st and the Niagara militia flank companies (with field-pieces) on the right. The Mohawk Indians, under Captain Norton, and a Niagara company of Blacks, proceeded along the brow of the mountain on the left, and the Light company of the 49th, with our company of militia broke through the centre. In this manner we rushed through the woods to the encamping ground on the Mountain which the enemy then occupied, and which had been the scene of their morning's success. The Indians were first in advance. As soon as they perceived the enemy they uttered their terrific war-whoop, and rushing rapidly upon them, commenced a most destructive fire. Our troops instantly sprung forward from all quarters, joining in the shout. The Americans gave a volley, then retreated tumultuously, and fled by hundreds down the Mountain. At that moment Captain Bullock and one hundred and fifty of the 41st, and two flank companies of militia appeared advancing on the road from Chippewa. The consternation of the enemy was complete. Though double in number, they stopped not to withstand their pursuers, but fled with the utmost precipitation. Never were men more miserably situated. They had no place to retreat to, and were driven by a furious and avenging enemy, from whom they had little mercy to expect, to the brink of the Mountain which overhangs the river. They fell in numbers—the river presented a shocking spectacle, filled with poor wretches, who plunged into the stream from the impulse of fear, with scarcely the prospect of being saved. Many leaped down the side of the Mountain to avoid the horrors which pressed on them, and were dashed to pieces by the fall. The fire from the American batteries ceased.

Two officers were now seen coming up

the hill with a white flag, and with some difficulty the slaughter was suspended. They were conducted up the Mountain to General Sheaffe. A cessation of hostilities for three days was asked for, and assented to. Thus, about four p.m., ended the business of this day, so important to the inhabitants of this Province. The invasion of our peaceful shores by its unprincipled neighbours, has terminated in the entire loss of their army, with everything brought over, not excepting their standards, with the very modest device of the Eagle perched upon the globe.

We have taken over nine hundred prisoners, with sixty of their officers. Except the wounded men, who were carried over in their boats, while they retained possession of the Mountain, scarcely a man has straggled back to relate to his country the disastrous event of an expedition planned by their unrighteous government.

The view of dead bodies which strewed the ground, and the mangled carcasses of poor suffering mortals, who filled every room in the village, filled us with compassion.

Still have we much to sorrow for, we

have a loss to deplore which the most brilliant success cannot atone for. That general, who led our army to victory, whose soul was wrapped up in our prosperity, is now shrouded in death.

Lieutenant-Colonel McDonell, too. This heroic young man, the constant attendant of the General, after his fall, strove to support to the last a cause never to be despaired of, because it involved the very salvation of his country.

But he was not destined to witness its triumph. His career was short but honourable; his end was premature, but full of glory.

He will be buried at the same time with the General.

Private William McKay

William McKay served in the York Militia, and possibly in the Lincoln Militia, during the War of 1812.

August 7th, 1812.

We slept under the trees on the bank of the river, arose early and set off. We did not land until we came to Patterson's Creek, about forty miles from the Grand River. Here we were informed that the volunteers from York, some of the 41st Regiment and some militia lay there that were to go with us.

August 8th, 1812.

Slept on shore in the best manner we could. Two of our company deserted this morning, James Bycraft and Harvey Thome. We did not leave this place until 12 o clock, when we set off and came to Long Point in the evening, drew our boats across and put up for the night.

August 9th, 1812.

Arose early this morning and about sunrise were joined by General Brock and six boat loads with troops from Patterson's Creek. We all set off together, having a fair wind till about one o'clock, and then rowed till night, when we landed at Kettle Creek, about six miles below Port Talbot.

August 10th, 1812.

Wet and cold last night; some of us lay in boats and some on the sand. We set off early, but the wind blew so hard we were obliged to put into Port Talbot. We covered our baggage from the rain, which still continued, and most of us set out to get something to eat, being tired of bread and pork. Five of us found our way to a place, where we got a very good breakfast, bought some butter and sugar and returned. Lay here all day, the wind being high.

August 11th, 1812.

Set off early with a fair wind, but it soon blew so hard we had to land on the beach and draw up our boats, having come twelve or fifteen miles. Some of us built camps and covered them with bark to shelter us from the rain, which poured down incessantly, but I was obliged to go on guard, wet as I was. Some of our men discovered horse tracks a few miles above us, which we supposed were American horsemen, for we were informed they came within a few miles of Port Talbot.

August 12th, 1812.

We set off before daylight and came on until breakfast time, when we stopped at Point 1 where we found plenty of sand cherries. They are just getting ripe and very good. We continued our journey all night, which was very fatiguing, being so crowded in the boats we could not lie down.

August 13th, 1812.

We came to a settlement this morning, the first since we left Port Talbot. The inhabitants informed us the Americans had all retired to their own side of the river, also that there was a skirmish between our troops and them on their own side, that is, the American side of the river. We made no stop, only to boil our pork, but kept on until two o'clock, when we lay on the beach until some of the boats with the General went on.

August 14th, 1812.

We landed at Fort Malden about eight o'clock, very tired with rowing, and our faces burned with the sun until the skin came off. Malden is about two miles from the lake, up the river, in which there are several small islands. The banks are low and well cultivated near the river, but a wilder ness back from it. Our company was marched to the storehouse, where we took out our baggage and dried it and cleaned our guns; were paraded at eleven o'clock and all our arms and ammunition that were damaged were replaced. We then rambled about the town until evening, when all the troops that were in Amherstburg were paraded on the commons. They were calculated at eight or nine hundred men.

The North West Rebellion

The North West Rebellion was a violent, five month long insurgency against the Canadian government, fought mainly by Métis and their First Nations allies in what is now Saskatchewan and Alberta, but was then a far frontier. The 12th Regiment, York Rangers and the Simcoe Foresters were each detailed to provide four companies for service in the North West. The York Rangers formed their four companies by combining the existing ones: Newmarket and Sharon, Aurora and Sutton, Yorkville and Seaton Village, and Parkdale and Riverside.

Captain J.F. Smith

J.F. Smith joined the 12th Regiment, York Rangers in June, 1875. He commanded Number 7 (Aurora) Company during the North West Rebellion.

Jack Fish Bay
April 8th, 1885

We are resting here today, in the first place to let the 6th Mounted Rifles get out of our way, and secondly our men need rest, for such a day we had yesterday I shall never forget. I never put in but one harder day in my life and that when the 30th marched from St Johns to La Prairie, you have heard me tell of it. The men stood remarkably well. Twenty-one miles in the pouring rain on the ice on the shore of Lake Superior, snow and slush nearly to the knees. We marched with water-proof sheets over our overcoats, of course Lick and Q.M. Collett rode with the baggage. I am sure there was a quart of water in each man's boots; I wore my top boots, I have got them well broken in and greased a couple of times, but nothing would turn 21 miles of snow water. We have not seen or heard one word of news since we left Toronto. We are totally ignorant of what is going on outside of ourselves, and we don't expect to hear a word 'til we get to Port Arthur or Winnipeg; we expect to reach that place about next Sunday or Monday. I suppose you know what we are doing better than I can tell you, you can hear of us but we cannot hear a word of you. Such a country as we have passed through I could never imagine could exist; snow and cold, why you don't know anything of it down there. Link and Mr. Collett are in the best of spirits and quite well. Major Ward of the 55th has a little boy, just the age of Charlie—and his name is Charlie—with him as a bugler, and I tell you he is a bugler, he served a term of training at the school.

Thursday, the hardest day I ever saw in my life, we made two portages and 50 miles on flat cars; we marched altogether about 25 miles, 15 of which was done in the dead of the night, up to our knees in snow and slush, but this is the last march. We are all perfectly well. I will write you again, so good bye to you all.

J.F. Smith

[The following letter was published in the Aurora Banner regarding Captain Smith]

Humboldt, N.W.T.
May 24th, 1885

To the Editor of the Banner

Dear Sir,

We the undersigned non-commissioned officers, on behalf of the company, having heard that a rumour had been circulated in Aurora about Captain Smith using his company harshly; we all wish to deny it. No officer could possibly have done more for his men than did our Captain during the whole trip. He always saw his own men as comfortably quarters as possible before he ever thought of his own comfort. We hope this will stop all "cackling" as we do not like to bear it. Thanking you for your valuable space.

Signed on behalf of and in the presence of the whole company.

Q.M. Sgt Chas. Collett
Col. Sgt W.H. Taylor
Segt. Barry Price
Segt. Donald Edge

Corp. Montgomery
Corp Hand
Segt. Farr, Military Police
Joseph Pugh, Orderly

Colour Sergeant W.H. Taylor

W.H. Taylor joined the 12th Regiment, York Rangers as a Private, and in 1908 was commissioned. He served in Number 7 (Aurora) Company during the North West Rebellion, and later commanded the company as a Captain.

April 10th, 1885

Dear Father and Mother,

I write you a few lines, as I thought you would like to know how we are getting along. We are having a very good time. We are over the worst part of the road. The worst of it is that sometimes we don't get more than two meals a day. We have already walked 50 miles. There is no snow along here. We left Port Arthur at 10 a.m. today, and will be in Winnipeg some time tomorrow. I like the trip splendidly. It is not so cold as it was when I wrote before. We had a forty mile sleigh ride on Easter Sunday, and on Tuesday we marched 22 miles over Lake Superior. The scenery was grand. I am well, and hope you are the same.

From your son,
Col-Sgt Taylor

The Second Boer War

Fought between 1899 and 1902, soldiers from across the British Empire were brought to South Africa to fight against Boer guerrillas of the Transvaal and the Orange Free State. This was the first foreign war in which Canadian troops participated.

Lieutenant Colonel T.H. Lloyd

T.H. Lloyd was commissioned as an Ensign in the York Militia in 1871, and commanded the 12th Battalion from 18999 to 1903. He served as a private soldier during the Fenian Raids in 1866. On September 6th, 1899, LCol Lloyd volunteered the entire 12th Battalion for service in South Africa. Although the original correspondence is lost, the reply is reprinted below.

Toronto, 29th September, 1899
From DOC, MD, No. 2
To
The Officer Commanding 12th Battalion

12th Battalion
Offer of Services
for South Africa

Referring to your letter of the 16th instant, upon the subject named in the margin, I am instructed to forward for your information and action, a copy of the remarks of the General Officer Commanding viz.

2. The Major general Commanding will have much pleasure in forwarding the letter of the Officer Commanding 12th Battalion, in which he offers the battalion under his command in aid of the Imperial Government in the Transvaal.

3.　The Major General Commanding cannot refrain from expressing his satisfaction at the patriotic feeling shown by Lieut-Col Lloyd and those under his command.

4.　I am desired to request that Lieut-Col Lloyd will be good enough to give the exact numbers of the non-commissioned officers and men who are actually prepared to volunteer for service.

It appears to the Major General Commanding that the statement that the whole regiment is prepared to volunteer may not be in accordance with the feeling of every individual connected with the battalion.

By order
H. Foster, Col, C S O

Corporal T.H. Graham

Harry Graham was a member of B Company, the 12th Regiment, York Rangers. He was one of nine Rangers who are known to have served in the Boer War, in his case with the Royal Canadian Regiment. His letters home were reprinted in the Aurora Banner.

Belmont Camp
Orange Free State, South Africa
Jan 21st, 1900

We are now stationed at this place and are having all we want of active service in South Africa with the Imperial troops. It is the hottest and sandiest place I ever saw. The thermometer stood 116 in the shade today and the wind blows strong every day and then the sand blows until our eyes and every part of us are full. Every few days a cyclone strikes the camp and clears a road through the camp like a race horse. I am nearly black with the heat and sand. There is no vegetation from here to Cape Town, over 700 miles nothing but sand and rock and I would not give $1000 for the whole country. The regiment is dead tired of it and all crazy to get home out of this miserable place. I weigh 170 lbs now but will soon be poor again for we are getting so much hard drilling.

We have a route march of over 20 miles per day and then we get up at 3 o'clock and line in the trenches till 6 o'clock for fear the Boers should make an early attack. We are camped on the old Belmont battlefield and the Boers never buried their dead men or horses and we have to do duty there and you can imagine the smell.

We have heard that they are going to send us home in March or first of April and I hope they do. They are going to send us by way of England and keep us there for a week. I suppose you heard about our little scrap at Douglas and Jacobadal. We never lost a man but the New Zealanders lost 4 men and 5 wounded. We looted a store and got its contents including hats, clothes and fruit, we also got 7 turkeys and 10 hens and our section ate them. It was a hard time for us in the heat and sand. I was so dry that my tongue swelled up and I could hardly speak. We were nearly choked for water.

Write soon and tell me all the news, we get very little news of the war here, they will tell us nothing.

Modder River
Sunday, Feb 18th, 1900

We arrived at Paardeburg Drift at 5:30 a.m. after doing a force march of 26 miles. On our arrival we were told that the Boers, 14,000 strong, under their leader Oronje were entrenched in the banks of the river two miles upstream, and that an engagement was in progress. We were also told that our Battalion would be in the engagement in a very short time. We could already hear the booming of the artillery, and see the British running to take positions on the neighbouring kopjes and knew that a great battle was in progress.

We were given thirty minutes for breakfast but it only took us fifteen minutes, for we were anxious to get at them. We were soon on parade again and were marched to protect the Howitzers and Field Artillery, but were ordered to retire half a mile and ford the river, six feet deep with a very swift current. We crossed the river in fours, with our kit and rifle high above our heads to keep them dry, and formed up in column on the right bank of the river, pretty wet as you can imagine.

We were now about two miles from the enemy's position, and were marched in extended order, the right half of the battalion in the attack and the left half in reserve. When we were 1000 yards from their position we extended to two paces and as we advanced we extended until within 600 yards from their position, when each man in advanced independently, under cover as much as possible, but the cover was very poor as we are on the level veldt.

We were now in line with ten thousand of the Imperial troops and we opened fire independently and continued firing till four o'clock, when a charge, led by the Canadians, was made, which proved so disastrous to our regiment. We were unsuccessful in the charge, so took cover 150 yards from the enemy and continued firing until we were compelled by the darkness to stop. The moon soon came up, however, and as the Boers had retreated two miles up the river to their laager, thus giving us a chance to look after our dead and wounded. I shall never forget the sight.

The cries and moans of the wounded would shake the nerves of the strongest heart but we had our painful work to perform and so continued all night searching for our boys among all the other dead and wounded. We took all the wounded to an old barn and used It for a hospital that night and the next day they were taken to the Brigade Field Hospital.

Next day, Monday the 19th, we picked up our dead, 26 in number, and buried them under a wild thorn tree on the battlefield. We buried all the poor fellows in one grave, without a coffin or shroud only the soldiers' uniform of khaki. Father O'Leary officiated as chaplain. We put up a headboard with the names of the heroes on it. Our casualties were 26 dead and 84 wounded.

We had no sleep for three days and night and had marched over 25 miles for three successive nights and had been on half rations for ten days, so we were nearly exhausted, still we did our duty. We were under fire two days and one night. Besides this we suffered something terribly from the heat during the day's battle, for we were lying prostrate on the red-hot sand all day and no sooner did we get dried from the wetting we got in fording the river than a heavy thunder storm came pelting down upon us and we were wet through again then the sun came out very hot and we just steamed.

We could not stand up to rest for to do so meant to lose your block, so we had to endure it. I'll continue this next week if I can possibly find time.

Private Harold Machin

Harold Machin was a member of B Company, the 12th Regiment, York Rangers. He was one of nine Rangers who are known to have served in the Boer War, in his case with the Royal Canadian Regiment. His letter home was reprinted in the Aurora Banner.

Orange River
16th Feb, 1900

I have just been discharged from hospital here having been laid up with fever, otherwise I would have written before to thank you and my Aurora friends for the gift [of $25 dollars] they sent me through you. The money itself is useful and appreciated, but what I feel more is the expression of good-will and patriotism which prompted you all in making Brunton, Graham and myself the subjects of a public expression of kindness itself. I never thought I had such friends and I assure you that when I think of all the kind things that have been said to me since leaving for South Africa, I long to be back so that I may meet my friends face to face and tell them how their kindness has touched me. Their good opinion and esteem is more to me than their gold, although, I admit, the latter in this instance came in handy. You must pardon my brevity, but as I am still very weak I'll have to stop. I will deal more fully when I return. From the bottom of my heart I thank you all and with kindest regards and best wishes to all Aurora and Newmarket friends.

The First World War

The British declaration of war against Germany on 4 August, 1914, automatically brought Canada into the war as well. With a Regular Army of only 3000 soldiers, the country relied heavily on its militia, both as a fighting force and to train the over six hundred thousand volunteers who stepped forward. It has been suggested that Canada truly emerged as a nation after the Battle of Vimy Ridge in 1917. The modern Regiment perpetuates four battalions of the Canadian Expeditionary Force: the 20th, 35th, 127th and 220th.

Honorary Colonel Leslie Frost

Leslie Frost joined the Canadian Expeditionary Force in 1916, and was transferred to the 20th Battalion in 1917. He was discharged in the rank of Captain due to wounds received in France in 1918. He later served as the Honorary Colonel of the Queen's York Rangers. In his civilian career he was a lawyer, a member of Provincial Parliament and later Premier of Ontario.

In the field
1 October 1917

Dear Dad & Mater,

I am back now after the Corps rifle match, arriving last Wednesday. I certainly had a good time. When I got back, I found the greatest bunch of letters and papers it has ever been my privilege to see, including a box – the birthday cake, which I was very glad to get. We had it for tea on night and it came in alright. There were two long letters from Dad and two from Mater. I was very interested in the sale of the house. I am glad it is sold and off your hands but do go someplace this winter where you will be comfortable. Don't live over the store. That is an awful place and there are no conveniences. I sure wish you would take a trip to Florida or Bermuda. It would do you both good.

I am anxiously waiting to get those snapshots you both have been speaking of an will be glad when they come.

I got a letter from Grandy the other day. He is "fed up" where he is and says he is going to work himself out the first draft he can. I don't blame him. England is certainly better in many ways than here but a fellow is never satisfied there. This place agrees with me. I am gaining weight and feel fine. Where we are now—the company officers (6 in number) are living in a dugout about 20' x 10'. We have fixed it all up. Built couches our of sandbags and have hung empty sandbags down the walls to keep the sand from falling down. After reading a lot of my newspapers, we have used the, for the same thing. We have a sort of fireplace and we are far from uncomfortable—as comfort goes out here. We have a fine bunch of officers in our company (C) and we have a happy time.

There has been some aerial activity around here of late and I saw our fellows bring down a Hun machine. These aviators certainly have lots of nerve.

Dad was mentioning about me reverting [to Lieutenant] to get out here, Well I do miss my captaincy to a degree but I would rather be out here as a private doing my bit than in England as a Colonel. The jobs in England can be quite well handled by casualty officer i.e. officers who have been wounded or rendered unfit for service in France. In the army, there is a growing feeling against officers who have not been to France holding down so-called soft jobs in England. Sooner or later it will come to a showdown there and they will either be forced to return home or come to France (reverting, of course). In fact, I believe that steps have already been taken in that direction. I am still being credited with Captain's pay but no doubt that will be changed. IN any case, I am not worrying and I will take a chance on getting my rank back, though it generally takes quite a long time. There are other senior officers who have reverted in the Battalion—some who could hardly afford to. I hear that the officers who return home without coming to France get rather a cool reception. I have met a lot of fellows from one old Battalion and they are all ore on Potter Robinson etc. for going back. It isn't a new thing to lose the rank but I think it was the right way to do it and it was the only way to get to France. If I had come home without coming here, I would have been in a nice position when I went back to Orillia, wouldn't I?

There is lots I could tell if I could, but it will all have to keep. Am greatly interested in the political situation in Canada—Stirring times, aren't they, in all parts of the world? Will write again soon.

Much love,
Leslie

GREAT NORTH WESTERN TELEGRAM

Sincerely regret inform you Lieut Leslie Miscampbell Frost Infantry officially reported wounded march thirty nineteen eighteen.

Director of Records

GREAT NORTH WESTERN TELEGRAM

Wounded not seriously prince wales hospital London.

—Frost

London
Sunday 7 April 1918

Dear Dad & Mater

Long before this you will have received my cable and also letters from Chaplains, the Red Cross etc. and you will know I have been wounded.

I was hit a week ago today—Easter Sunday March 31st about 7:30PM. The bullet went through both thighs but nothing serious—no bones broken.

Arrived in England April 4th and am at:

The Prince of Wales Hospital for Officers
Marlybone Road
London, N.W.

Am getting along fine and hope to be better soon. Address my letters to:

Royal Bank of Canada
2 Bank Buildings
Princes St
London ECR

And they can forward it on wherever I am. Hope Mater is better and that you are both well.

Much love,
Leslie

Prince of Wales Hospital
14 April 1918

Dear Dad & Mater,

Another week has passed an I am on the road to be quite better. I am feeling fine and have a good appetite etc. The wounds are healing and in a week or ten days I should be able to get up. The stiffness has left my wounds and the only thing that bothers me at all is a nerve in my left foot but time will fix that alright. The wound in the left leg is practically healed and it has never hurt in the least but it affected in some way the muscle on the very bottom of my foot and for a time the back of my leg but that has gone.

I am sending you the "Times" which has my name in the casualty list. I thought you would like to see it.

Heber Greene has been in to see me several times. He is the Canadian chaplain for Canadians in London Hospitals.

I was notified this week that have been reposted to a unit in England so I will have my mail sent there and they can send it on to me. That is part of their job. I now belong to the 1st Central Ontario Regimental Depot.

I hope everything is OK at home. I am anxious to get my mail from France. Hope you are both well. Will write soon.

With love,
Leslie

Private Clifford Carter

Clifford Carter served in the 20th Battalion, C.E.F. in the Grenadier Platoon of 'C' Company. He wrote a number of letters to the editor of his hometown newspaper, the *Burlington Gazette*. He was killed on 13 August, 1916, when a grenade detonated accidently in his hand during training, and is buried in the Ridge Wood Military Cemetery, Belgium.

In Billets Somewhere in Belgium, Oct. 4, 1915

Just a line from the boys from Burlington. We have received our first baptism of fire, as we have had a spell in the trenches, but are now out in reserve billets for a little rest. We can still hear the crack of the rifles and machine guns, and are easily within range of the guns, if they desired to move us. I have just been watching the flares the mines are sending up. They illuminate the front nearly all night. It rained all the time we were in the trenches, and as a matter of fact, it rains nearly all the time over here. We have had a white frost or two, making it kind of chilly at night.

All the boys are well. I suppose you know that Geo. Graham was left in England, owing to the fact that he had hardly recovered from his sickness, but the rest of us are all together yet.

Somewhere in Belgium.

Just a line to say that the boys from Burlington are still alive and well. We have just come out of rest after 18 days in the trenches. Winter is setting in but it is not at all Canadian, as it is wet all the time. The trenches are in pretty bad shape, but others are being built, so we do not expect to live in water all winter.

Some reinforcements have just joined us, and I learn from them that George Graham has a staff job in England. He is a lucky one. I am enclosing a sketch by E. G. Green, of the R.C.D.'s in which he pictures Jack Lardie on the march.

Well, I must close, wishing you good luck and best wishes from the boys of Burlington.

Flanders, November 15th.

Here's for a line to say that the Burlington boys in the 20th are still alive and well.

It is true, we had a little scrap the other day, but am glad to say all came through safe.

At present we are in billets further behind the line that we have ever been since first going into the trenches, just seven months ago. Believe me it is quite a relief to be away from the guns, especially the Fritz'.

I am sending you under separate cover, a copy of the March edition of our Regimental Gazette, which is edited in the trenches each month. Without a doubt you will find a few items worth reproducing, and you have the editors' permission to do so at your own will. I have no news just now, except that all are well.

Somewhere in Belgium, Nov. 20th, 1915

Here's a line to say that we received the copies of your paper, and believe me, on behalf of the boys, I send many thanks, for we sure appreciated their arrival. May I ask you, through the medium of your columns, to thank the Queen's Canadian Military Hospital Committee for the tobacco which they so kindly sent us. The majority of us received it O.K. about 5 weeks ago.

Oh say, don't forget to reproduce that sketch of Jack Lardie, as he would like the folks to see what our surroundings are when we are on the march. Well, we are out of the first line, and we are in reserve. We are working on our day shifts now, which is easier on us, as the trenches are in pretty bad shape, for it rains nearly every day, and the cold weather doesn't make it any more comfortable.

This last trip in we had a pretty tough time, for they shelled us pretty heavily. On the 18th of Nov. we lost our first Halton rifleman in our battalion, in the person of Private. G. McLeod, of Acton. He was given as nice a funeral and grave as possible under the conditions. He was sniped off, receiving two wounds, one bullet through the arm, which pierced his lung, and another in the groin. He was a good chum, and will be missed by all who met him.

Now for the bright side. We had the pleasure of hearing that a German taube and two officers had been captured just behind us. I have no more news except to say that E. Oakes, R. R. Wooding and myself are now in the Grenade Platoon, and all letters to us should be addressed that way instead of C. Co. I am pleased to say that all the boys from Burlington are well, and I hope you are the same.

Belgium, January 14th, 1916

At last I have found courage and time to write you. It is just 4 months to-day since we landed in Belgium, and we have been doing trench duty all the time. We expect to go back to a rest camp within the next two months. At last leave has started, but only a few at a time. For instance, in the Grenade Section, we have one man going on leave every Monday morning. There are 45 men in the Sec., so you see it will take about a year for us all to have leave. However, we expect that once we get a rest, there will be more going at a time.

I suppose you will ask what I think of the war and active service. Well, to tell you the truth, I wouldn't give a care if it finished to-day. For there is nothing beautiful in dodging bullets and whizz-bangs, and living in the mud.

The rain fall out here is fierce. It's raining every day, and the mud is terrific.

Our lines are in pretty good shape, but they were fierce when we took them over. It has meant a terrible amount of work and material to fix them up. And a few lines, for there are quite a few of the old boys gone.

However, duty first. Our lines are from 75 to 250 yards from the Germans' 1st line. Just a nice range for our grenade guns, and believe me, we do some nice work once in a while.

At present we are in billets a couple of miles behind the line, for a few days. We were out for a route march to-day, and then tactical exercise, just to show the Brigadier how we would make a charge.

Well, I must close, hoping this will reach you all in the best of health. Please give my best wishes to all my old friends. Good bye for now.

Captain Stuart Kirkland

Stuart Kirkland enlisted in the 91st Battalion in St Thomas, Ontario, but was transferred to the 35th Battalion upon arrival in England. Wounded at Vimy Ridge, he was returned to Canada where he served until the end of the war. In civilian life, he was a barrister.

17th August, 1916

I thought I would take advantage of a rainy Sunday afternoon to write some letters. There are so many persons around Dutton, however, to whom I would like to write but cannot for lack of time, that I thought I would write you a good long epistle and you make what use of it you think best.

Just as I finished that opening paragraph an aeroplane flew past, making an unusual amount of noise and I went to the tent door to look at it. It was flying very low - did not appear to be more than 150 feet high. Aeroplanes as a rule excite very little curiosity here, as there are dozens of them flitting pasty every day. Sometimes you can hear them but cannot see them when they are very high up and it is cloudy. They make a noise exactly like a saw mill in full operation.

The camp where I am quartered is known as West Sandling, and there are four regiments here - the 12th, 25th, 36th and 39th reserve battalions. I suppose that you have already head that "Elgin's Pride" has been broken up. There is no 91st any longer. I am now attached to A Company of the 35th, the battalion which reinforces the 19th and 20th battalions at the front from time to time. I was fortunate in being placed in an excellent battalion. It is a Toronto unit and commanded by Lieut.-Col. McCordick. Of course, I was sorry to know that conditions required the breaking up of our 91st, but I will have to make the best of things. I am very sorry though that the rest of the Dutton boys are not with me. The majority of them were sent with C. Company to the 36th battalion. As they are in the same brigade, however, I will see them often, at least up to the time we got to France or Belgium.

By the way, Sergeant Harry Locke in the 36th and I have had several talks with him. He came back from the front but is quite alright again and has been placed in the 36th. He will likely go back to the firing-line with an early draft. He looks splendid but has grown a big busy moustache and I would never have known him to meet him on the street. (I say in parenthesis we are under strict orders that the upper lip must not be shaved and I am getting a moustache myself which, with careful cultivation, is going to be a "beaut.") Sergeant Locke has been awarded the military medal for gallantry at the front. He was one of those in the First Canadian Division upon whom the honor was conferred on the occasion of the King's birthday. I want the people of Dutton to know this, for they should be proud of Harry.

I have run across several other boys who used to be around Dutton. In this part of Kent there are none but Canadian troops. They flock the towns around and if you go into Folkestone or Hythe in the evening you are sure to meet someone who you know. It was in Folkestone I met Lieut. Lyal Kennedy. He is trying for a transfer to the Royal Flying Corps. I also met Billy Crehan, formerly of Wallacetown, who was attending Toronto University and is expecting a commission in the Imperial Army. Another man who is well known in Dutton and whom I meet often at mess, is Major Tolmie, of

Windsor, paymaster of the (former) 99th. I was chatting with him a few minutes before I started this letter.

This county, (Kent) is very beautiful, with its quaint old towns, thatched roofs, hedgerows and hop fields. I wish you could see it. The only unpleasant feature is the rain. It seems to drizzle here about every other day and it always seems damp and raw. You could wear an overcoat almost any day without being uncomfortable. But perhaps I am judging the climate too hastily for the past two or three days have been really warm and pleasant and I hope it may continue that way for a while.

When there is a heavy bombardment on around Zeebrugge or at the west of the battle line at Dunkirk, or in the direction of Ypres, we can distinctly hear the rumble of the big guns. You know we are only a few miles from Dover, and from Dover to Calais across the channel is only a little over 20 miles. I thought at first the noise I heard was thunder but as I was hearing it every morning at made enquiries and was told it was the noise of battle.

I have not had a chance to see much of England yet but hope to get a few days leave before long and will got up to London, which is only about 70 miles from here, for a few days. The things that impressed me most however in the short time I have been here are there:

(1) The almost total absence of able bodied me in civilian dress. You see nothing but soldiers everywhere. Only an occasional man is noticed in civilian attire and he is either an old man or medically unfit. All the classes from 19 to 41 have been called out and are under arms. The trains are crowded with men in khaki, the streets throng with them - they are everywhere.

(2) The way in which women are taking up man's place in all departments. It looks odd to see a woman perched on the driver's seat on a hack or driving a taxi, but that is the everyday thing here now.

(3) The antediluvian make-up of the big English newspapers. I am not saying this to flatter the publishers of The Advance. But I must say that in general make-up the papers here are a hundred years behind the times. The editorials are beautifully written. The English is superb and all that,

but so far as news is concerned you have to search very carefully to find it and you generally find that really interesting items (war news, etc.,) carefully concealed in some remote corner on a back page. The front page is usually given up to ads and even these are of the most commonplace and lack the snap and ginger that a Canadian or an American puts into his advertisements. Isn't "display" the technical term for what I mean? Well, then, English newspapers are away behind in that respect.

I would like to tell you something about our voyage over in the Olympic but I must not take too much of your time. There were over 6000 troops with us and the trip was delightful. The great ocean liner is certainly a leviathan. I got lost whenever I tried to go anywhere in it. It rides the waves beautifully and hardly anyone was at all sick.

I think perhaps the most beautiful sight I have ever seen was the Isle of Man as it appeared from deck. It was something to always remember. We got glimpses of the shores of Ireland and Scotland, too, but were not close enough to see them clearly. As we sailed up the Mersey past Birkinhead and into Liverpool the scene was a busy one. The boats flitting about, the tremendous shipping, the busy docks, wouldn't give you the impression that old England was at war at all. I may say I got a glimpse of the Mauretania in Liverpool Harbor.

I would also like to talk about Hythe and Folkestone, the only large towns I have seen here yet besides Liverpool, but I must stop. I may say before closing that Folkestone is a summer resort town of about 35,000 population and it is very interesting to the Canadian visitor. Just now you see more Canadian soldiers there than anyone else, but there is also a big sprinkling of French and Belgium officers on the street. Next time I write I will try to tell you more and to make my letter more interesting. I am afraid this one has been rather prosy and I know it is decidedly ill-written.

With best regards to all my Dutton friends.

The Second World War

Canada's contribution to the war, lasting from 1939 to 1945, was even greater than that during the First World War. The Canadian Army had been allowed to atrophy between the wars, forcing a massive program of training and rebuilding to occur once again. The Queen's York Rangers, now designated a machinegun regiment, were employed on security duties within Canada, and as a training organization to feed soldiers into other units. Altogether, the Regiment trained over 2000 soldiers who went on to serve in other units.

Pilot Officer Albert Wallace

Al Wallace was a Private in the Queen's York Rangers prior to World War Two, transferring to the Royal Canadian Air Force in 1940. He served with 419 Bomber Squadron, flying over Germany and occupied Europe.

Before the war I joined Queen's York Rangers as a Private, fitting in militia training weekends around his job in a Toronto Loblaw's. When Parliament declared war on Germany on September 10, 1939, all my friends and I reported to Fort York Armoury, ready for what we assumed would be a trip overseas with the rest of the Canadian Army. But we were wrong: instead, after weeks of drill, administration, and issuing of what little kit the regiment had, I found himself bound for the Niagara Peninsula.

We got put on a bus and the next thing we knew we were on guard duty along the Welland Canal. We were walking back and forth along the banks of the canal, and I don't even know what lock it was we were guarding. It was dark and we had a rifle each, our uniforms, but no bullets – they didn't give us any bullets for some reason.

I was only there for a week, then we got back on the bus and we're back in

Toronto and they tell us to go back to our jobs. And that was it for the Queen's York Rangers, all the excitement was over."

I mean we were all kids, we had uniforms but that was pretty much it. I have no idea why they thought the Welland Canal was going to be attacked, but it was only for a week. The big worry while we were guarding it was that one of us would fall in – it was pretty dark at night and it got foggy too, so I was seriously concerned about falling in.

I was part of the machine-gun crew: I was the range finder. We used to practice on the armoury floor with the Vickers gun on a tripod: I would lay on the floor and tell the guy behind the gun what the range to the target was.

The biggest excitement I got was when we went to the Long Branch range and I got to sit behind the Vickers machine-gun and fire, I think it was about 20 rounds. That was fun, because I've always been a gun lover – I still am.

The Rangers never went active, for the whole war, and if they had ever gone active I would've gone overseas with them. But they never did, so I went back to my job at Loblaw's and I tried to join the Air

Force. Well, they told me they couldn't touch me because I was in the Army, and I had to get a discharge. So, I said, that's fine and I went in and got my official discharge: they sent me a printed certificate, that was framed and everything.

I wanted to join the RCAF, because my best friend at the time was in the RCAF, so I went into the recruiting office and they signed me up. When I joined, they made me a "GD" – general duties – and that's about as low as you can go in the air force.

I spent the next year or so at No. 1 Bombing and Gunnery School, in Jarvis, Ont., just outside Hamilton, sweeping out hangars and doing odd jobs: whatever needed to be done. We spent most days out watching the bombing range on Fort Erie, plotting where all the practice bombs fell and radioing back the results.

Eventually, I got promoted to Corporal and posted to the Ground Instruction School at Jarvis, where I was in charge of handing out the machine-guns to the bomb aimers and the air gunners who were being trained at the school, so I got to know the Lewis and the Vickers guns pretty well.

Then one day a posting came through: they were looking for air gunners in the worst way over in England, so right away I put my name in and I got accepted within a few weeks and started my training there in 1942.

I graduated, then it was off to Halifax to wait for our troopship to come in: and it was the Queen Elizabeth: the biggest ocean liner in the world. While I was in Halifax, I got promoted to Pilot Officer and I had to go to the tailor to get an officer's uniform, and all that junk – I wasn't too happy about that. All my friends from the school were sergeants and corporals, and they were staying down in the hold. I was up in a cabin, with four other officers.

We landed in Scotland and took the train down to Bournemouth, on the south coast, which was where all the Canadian aircrew who were in England got sent. I was there about six weeks and I got a phone call – it was a friend of mine from Toronto, was with a squadron up in Yorkshire and he had a crew for a Halifax bomber that didn't have a mid-upper gunner. He knew I was a mid-upper gunner and that I had just arrived in

England so he got his CO to get through all the red tape and send me a ticket to Yorkshire. I went up there, met all the guys, shook everyone's hand and that's how I became their air gunner on 411 Squadron, which was a Canadian squadron.

They told me that there was no room for me in the officer's quarters, so I'd have to stay in a Nissen Hut. Well, that was fine by me but it was cold as hell, because it was February. But I wasn't in there very long – maybe two weeks, because the squadron was already operational, and every night there were bombers that didn't come home. So pretty soon there were vacancies in the officer's quarters, because guys got shot down – they just disappeared.

Well, I didn't last too long either. I got there in February and I got the chop on May the 13th 1943 – I got in 15 air operations over Germany. Lots of tough missions, all over Germany, until I got the chop over Duisburg.

We lost two engines and the pilot's canopy was shattered, Mac [WO Glen McMillan of Maryfield, Sask.] had to put on goggles so he could see in all the wind.

There was a big hole in one wing and it caught fire: it looked like a huge blowtorch, so Mac gave the order to bail out over the intercom.

We were hit over the target, we think it was flak but it could've been a German aircraft – who knows? In the pitch darkness it was hard to tell for sure. I was the mid-upper gunner, and I used to sit up there on top of the world scanning all around me in my turret, but it was pitch black: you couldn't see anything. Any German night fighter out there could've seen us long before we saw them.

I sat there with my feet dangling out of the hatch in the slipstream, trying to work up the nerve to bail out. We were at about 19,000 feet when we got hit, and it was pitch black, and I just couldn't get the nerve to jump. So, I plugged into the intercom, and said: "Mac, how high are we?"

Because I had the idea in my head that if I jumped I was going to hit the ground before the parachute opened. So, Mac said: "We're at 12,000 feet and we're in real trouble Al; get out!"

So, I went back over to the hatch and sat down again with my feet in the slipstream; gave myself a little twitch and a wiggle and I was out: just like that. I already had my hand on the D-bar [ripcord], and we're supposed to wait three seconds before we pull it, but I didn't wait – soon as I was out, I pulled on the D-bar. It was pretty foolish actually, because the Halifax had a huge tail assembly and if that chute had caught on it I would've followed that plane right down to the ground.

So, there I am, hanging in the sky above the cloud level in complete, utter total darkness. Finally, I went through the cloud level and could see the horizon and I landed about 30 feet from a German farmer's barn. All the training came back to me, I bent my legs, folded and rolled when I hit the ground: but I was lucky that there wasn't any wind that night.

Two farmers had been watching me all the way down, because they'd seen the plane burning as it came down, so they walked up to me and collected me and took me inside their farmhouse. I guess they'd called the police or the army or something, because pretty soon two German soldiers in a motorbike showed up in about half an hour. They searched me, but the only thing they took was my Mae West: they didn't take my watch or anything.

They took me to the local police station, and that's where I met up with our bomb aimer [P/O Henry Enever, RAF] – we were both put into one of the cells. We were there about two hours, when a truck rolled up. They pulled us out of the cell and the guy from the truck, he whips his pistol out and waves it around in our faces to let us know if we tried anything funny, they'd shoot us. So, they put us in the back of the truck and there are two coffins in it ... just rough boards put together. And we weren't sure, but I think now that was our pilot and our wireless operator. Five of us got out of the aircraft; two didn't –Mac, the pilot, and the radio operator [Sgt Walter Alison, RAF]. Mac kept the plane level while the rest of us bailed out, he and Walt died when the plane hit the ground.

They took the coffins to a mortuary and we carried the coffins in, then got back on the truck. From there we went to a train station in Frankfurt, and the train took us to Gulag Luft – which was a small prison camp that only had one purpose: it was a German interrogation centre: the

Germans wanted to interrogate all the aircrew they captured, but I don't know what they wanted to find out.

They took me out into an office to be interrogated by an officer and he knew more about the war than I did. He knew more about our bombing squadron. I didn't have to tell him anything. He could tell me everything that they needed to know about our bombing. He told them who our commanding officer was and how many aircraft we could put up on a maximum effort and oh, he knew far more about the air base than I did.

I was only there for two weeks, then it was back on the train and that took me to Stalag Luft 3: the Great Escape camp [a Luftwaffe POW camp near Zagan, Poland]. It was a brand-new camp; it had only opened in April of 1943 and I was arriving in May. So, I was only there six weeks after it had opened. And it had about 700 or 800 men in it when I arrived, but it would eventually have about 1800 or 1900.

It was a big camp, double barbed wire fences around it, about ten feet apart, two fences. And then in between the two fences, there was great coils of barbed wire all around it to make it very difficult, literally impossible to get through. There were guard towers at different points all around the camp and they had machine guns in the towers and they had searchlights, which at night were on all night in the camp.

The camp was all air force personnel: mostly British, but Australians, South Africans, New Zealanders, a few French guys, and Norwegians, but there were more Canadians I think than any other nationality – aside from the British. I moved into a room in block 104, and block 104 was the barrack block where the big tunnel used in the Great Escape started. I didn't know it at the time, of course, because I was quite a newcomer. And everything about the escaping was very secretive in the camp and really wasn't talked about a great deal.

And in my view, it wasn't a very good room really to live in because when the tunnel was opened, there was blankets all over the floor to catch any sand and the room was in effect off limits, you couldn't go back and forth into it. So, I only was in that room for I think two to three months and then I made arrangements to move out of there.

I did do a little bit of work on the tunnel on the sand disposal. I was what we called a penguin - I had these long, thin sand bags down my trouser legs, filled with dirt from the tunnel and I disposed of it out in our garden outside our block or around the circuit that we walked, around the perimeter of the camp. But that was the only thing I did on the tunnel was a bit of sand disposal.

Everybody in the camp knew what was going to happen. That particular day they were going to break out or that night. Throughout the day, everybody in hut 104 moved out of that hut except the men that were going to be going out. When they opened the tunnel to the surface, they went up and they had some delays. They had a hard time breaking through the ground to the surface and when the tunnel opened, they found out that they had thought they were going to be within the pine trees around the camp. Well, they were about 20 feet short. But fortunately, they were about 30 feet behind one of the guardhouses. And the guardhouse was up there with a guard in it, of course, with a searchlight, but he was shining it into the camp, not out. So, he really wasn't a problem.

But the Germans also had guards on foot patrolling outside the main wire around the camp, so they arranged a timing and a rope: they had a rope in the camp that one of the men held and then one of them went out the tunnel and into the woods and when the guards had turned and they were walking away so they couldn't see, he would pull the cord and one or two men in the tunnel would jump out and into the woods. Well that way, they were able to get 76 guys out.

Well, I remember that night. I was laying in my bunk and I don't think I slept much because I knew the tunnel break was taking place and I just wondered when things were going to happen. Well, sure enough, I think around 5:00 in the morning, I heard a rifle shot, one single shot. And I said, oh, that's probably it. One of the guards had veered off towards the tunnel, he was going to have a leak, you see. And he nearly fell in the hole, he was so close to it. And just at that moment, the boys got their signals mixed up and one had pulled the cord in the woods and the one inside thought that was the clearance to pop out and he jumped out of the tunnel right in front of this guard and the guard, of course, I guess he must have been quite shocked, and so he whipped his rifle up and fired a shot. But he missed the man and so that was, from there, the escape was over.

There was 50 of the 76 that were shot and they were just murdered. I mean, they were taken out in small groups and just shot in the back of the head. That was how they went. The Germans didn't admit that, they just said that they were shot while trying to escape. And of course, our commanding officer, when he was told this said, "Well, how many were wounded?" "Well," the Germans said, "well, none, they were all killed." Well, I mean, that told them right away that they had been murdered. The camp all knew immediately that they had all been murdered and we all wore black bands there for several weeks afterwards to signify to the Germans that we knew what had happened.

That was a tough time around the camp because so many people had lost friends that were one of these 50 guys. A lot of them had been prisoners for three or four years and here they were, all of sudden, their lives blotted out, boom, like that. It was a tough time in the camp.

A few months later, we could tell the front was getting closer: we could see planes flying overhead, dropping bombs and even hear the shelling in the distance. So, the Germans decided to evacuate the camp. They marched us out at 12:30 at night and made us walk halfway across Germany – we were marching for more than a week, in the winter. A lot of guys bought it on that march, but one morning we woke up and the guards were gone: just disappeared. Then – I'll never forget it – an armoured car roars into the farmyard where we had spent the night and the hatch pops up and out comes a British officer. That was how we were liberated.

I have no regrets about my time in Germany: it was tough, I got shot down after all, but the Germans were by and large pretty decent to us.

Peacekeeping Operations

Although Lester Pearson's leadership in getting the United Nations to intervene in the 1956 Suez Crisis is often cited as the birth of peacekeeping, Canadian soldiers were involved in United Nations operations as early as 1948, when an observer force was dispatched to Kashmir. Since then, more than 125,00 Canadian Armed Forces members have served on international peacekeeping missions, and over 130 have died doing so.

Captain Ryerson Maybee

Ryerson Maybee joined the Regiment in 1994, commissioning in 2012. He has served on three overseas tours, twice to Bosnia and once to Afghanistan. In his civilian career, he is a security manager at the City of Mississauga.

Bosnia in 1998 was my first deployment overseas. For reservists it was always difficult to get a spot-on deployment. I had to compete against all of the other reservists in the battalion to get a position as a grenadier in a rifle company. Turns out that I got a spot after six months of work up training, with Para company of 3 RCR. I don't have jump wings. At the time the 40mm M203 was new to the inventory for Canada and thus I had never trained on it. I spent work up training with the signals platoon and was a last-minute addition to a section to replace another reservist who turned out to be unsuitable for the deployment. I turned in my "vanilla" C7 at Company Stores and drew one with a 203 on it just before terminal leave (the week or so you get before you actually deploy). I asked the CQ staff for a manual on the M203.

Fast forward several months and I've been living and working in Camp Maple

Leaf in Zgon Bosnia. The camp is an old textile factory and our "weatherhavens" are setup inside the main factory complex. The only things you would find in a normal battalion lines that were outside the main building were the CQ stores for each of the three sub units that took up space in Maple Leaf – A squadron from the Dragoons, and one from 2 CER, and Para coy from 3 RCR. It was a slow tour for the most part, presence patrolling along the inter- entity boundary line – the line decided in Dayton Ohio that demarcated where the Bosnian Serb controlled "Republic Srpska" began and Bosnia "proper" ended. We inspected some cantonments, did a couple of exercises but mostly just drove around and talked to people. One of the rotating tasks that each section in the platoon had to do was Quick Reaction Force – the section would be the immediate back up for any patrol in the Area of operations that was in trouble, or needed some extra hands. The QRF got called out so infrequently we jokingly referred to it as the "CQRF" due to the tendency of the Company Quartermaster using the QRF as his personal work party. Mostly it meant you had to stay in uniform, keep track of your movements on a white board, and not do much. Practically speaking that means we all got pretty good at foosball. QRF routine went like this:

- Get up
- Shave
- Do PT
- Briefing from our Sect Comd
- Get a coffee at the mess
- Load our kit on our Grizzly
- Do daily maintenance checks
- Start playing foosball

We wouldn't be stood down until all patrols for the day were in or the day ended (midnight) when a new section took over. And so it went for most days of the tour helping CQ do stuff or playing foosball and waiting for something to happen.

So, it was on the afternoon of Serbian new year, me and the mates playing foosball in the mess when the Sarge came in and said "We're being deployed".

We all looked at each other as though he was joking. One of the guys said: "Seriously Sarge?!"

He just shouted yes as he moved off at a shuffle to the CP and we all shrugged and ran out to the carrier. As we were firing up the Grizzly the Sergeant arrived with our Platoon Commander in tow.

"The Lt will be joining us for this move guys".

Our platoon commander was a short, aloof, sort of nerdy guy who this far into the tour hadn't had much to do with us. We traded knowing glances with each other and mounted up. I was the third in command on this outing and so was up through the family hatch in the back of the carrier with a headset on. The Platoon Commander popped up on the other side and told me to get him onto a headset as well. I arranged this with some grumbling – we had just the one spare and it meant moving kit around the interior of the Grizzly, which was a pain the ass at the best of times, much less on the move at 60km/h to an as yet unknown incident. The Sergeant had given us a quick brief before we left, another patrol from the platoon had spotted a vehicle with an armed individual in it, and was following. They needed us to block the road that they were on so we could effect a search, and hopefully seize the weapon. The Sergeant tried to update us as we moved, but with only two people in the back with headsets he missed a bunch.

We arrived at our intercept point, a small parking area in front of a shop and adjacent to the road our patrol was on. The driver and gunner remained mounted but the rest of us dismounted.

"Are we kitting up for this Sarge?" I asked. Our normal SOP was no frag vest, no load bearing vest for patrols and soft hats (usually our berets). All our fighting order stayed in the carriers. I carried my rifle ammo in my pockets – most of my section mates left it in their vests...which would be in the carrier if there was a fight.

The Sergeant looked at our Platoon Commander who was wearing his parka, and a pistol on his hip. He shook his head. We all shrugged.

"Maybee, put this on." The Sergeant handed me a bright orange vest with white reflective chevrons.

"Really?!" I replied.

He nodded, adding "We don't want you to get hit by a car."

My task was to halt the target vehicle. I removed the plastic plugs from my grenade launcher.

"What're you doing?" asked the Sergeant.

"If you take those out, they might think your launcher is loaded."

"Exactly" was my reply.

He shrugged and I put on the traffic vest ensuring that the Velcro fasteners were folded in and not secured. I was going to get that thing off me as soon as possible. I wasn't relishing being a target. The road itself was two narrow lanes of blacktop with a 2-foot ditch on the opposite side of where we had the carrier. The Grizzly was 90 degrees to the road so we would be able to cut the road easily when the time came. I stood at the edge of the ditch and noted that beyond it was a wire fence about five feet high.

I took a deep breath and played out the stop in my mind a couple of times – What if the car tries to run me down? Where will I go? Will I try to dodge it? Or should I shoot? My C7 was on a "patrol" sling which meant it hung across my body just above my waist, like all good soldiers I kept my dominant hand on my pistol grip, ensuring positive control of my weapon. I rehearsed swinging my left hand up in a "stop" gesture a couple of times to the amusement of my mates. I was ready.

Shortly after that a long line of vehicles could be seen coming over a small rise in the road with much honking and other noise making. Our target vehicle was a Volkswagen Rabbit. I had pictured it alone on the road racing away from our platoon mates Grizzly which would be in hot pursuit. I had forgotten it was Serbian new year. The impromptu parade of cars was in celebration of that event. The lead vehicle saw me and slowed, then it saw the carrier and the others of the section waiting and slowed even more. While my brain was still trying reconcile the imagined and the real I could see the other carrier from the platoon at the end of the long line of vehicles. Suddenly a vehicle pulled out of the long line into the oncoming lane and accelerated.

"Sarge here's our guy!" I shouted as a black VW Rabbit put two wheels off the road kicking up a rooster tail of wet grass and dirt as it sped toward me.

With all the resolve I possessed I raised my left hand in the rehearsed

"Stop" gesture and put my most stern "Halt" face on.

It had no effect.

I don't know if the car saw me and ignored me, or if they didn't notice the 23-year-old Corporal in the bright orange with reflective white chevron vest standing in their way. Regardless they hadn't slowed down at all.

Standing there I had a conversation with myself about how long I would wait before raising my weapon, when that threshold was reached I brought my rifle into my shoulder and reached for the cocking handle with my left, the windscreen filled my scope as I drew a bead on the driver, and suddenly I could see the roof of the vehicle as well. I lowered my weapon far enough to see over the sight and could see the front end of the car go down as he braked hard.

Our carrier hadn't moved.

I yelled again that this was our guy and at last the carrier jerked forward, just in time to clip the driver's side of the rabbit as it tried to manoeuvre around the carrier. The mirror of the rabbit popped off and sailed through the air. The car swerved violently to its right and stopped.

All four doors opened and four young men dismounted. I had flipped the traffic vest off by now and was advancing toward the car.

My fireteam partner was the Sergeant and he had both hands in the air in a "calm down gesture" with his sidearm still holstered. I scanned each of the men, they're aggressive, but no gun visible, wait one has something in his hand! I went back into the aim and realized it was a brown beer bottle...again I lowered my weapon and closed the distance between the four men and me.

The four now surrounded the Sergeant, but had calmed a little. Four of us now formed a loose cordon around the section commander and the car looking in to him and our interpreter trying to talk to the four angry men who had come out of the car.

With a great deal of surprise, I was shoved from behind. I stumbled forward to keep from losing my balance and whirled around to see a crowd of some hundreds flowing past the carrier to surround us all.

The people from the rest of the vehicles.

They shouted and gestured and swarmed around me. Keeping my weapon at waist level I swung in a semi-circle hitting a couple with the muzzle while shouting "back up!". Doing this I managed to clear about a meter's worth of space between me and the hostile crowd. Another young man, bespectacled, bearded moved to the front rank of the crowd.

"Are you going to shoot us?!"

"Not if everyone behaves, no."

"Then why are you pointing your gun at us!?!"

"Just back up and give us space"

"Stop pointing you gun at us! Then we'll back up."

Time slowed and a full-on debate with podiums, a moderator, cameras, and commentator play by play went on in my head. If I let go of the pistol grip and let my rifle hang it will take 0.738 seconds to grab it again...which will slow me down by about a second if I have to shoot one of these people...But if I let it hang I may de-escalate the situation and thus not have to shoot anyone...

I let go of the grip on my C7 and raised both hands in a "shove" motion.

"BACK UP."

The crowd complied and one meter turned into four, then five. I knew that we wouldn't find a weapon at this point. The crowd had surged up on all of us and someone no doubt grabbed it out of the car and moved it back to the line of vehicles on the other side of the carrier. We reversed out of the way and allowed traffic to flow again, the crowd dispersed. The four angry men got back into the rabbit after a short search that found nothing. I recovered the vest from the ditch where I'd tossed it and mounted back up into our Grizz. We didn't talk much on the way back to camp. I think we all felt as though we'd "lost" in the encounter. We'd been outsmarted by the crowd, and outmanned.

Still I'd learned a valuable lesson that would serve me not only on my two subsequent tours, but in life in general. My instincts were good, and if I trusted them I would be ok. We arrived back at camp and dismounted ready to do some maintenance and maybe drink a pop. Our Platoon Commander got out of the carrier and unzipped his parka. I saw fury pass over the Sergeant's face, and a moment later I saw why.

Underneath his parka our Platoon Commander was wearing his frag vest.

Lieutenant Colonel Phil Halton

Phil Halton began his military career in the Royal Canadian Dragoons, and commanded the Queen's York Rangers from 2012 to 2016. He served in Bosnia as a Reconnaissance Troop Leader on Operation PALLADIUM. In his civilian career, he is a novelist and screenwriter.

Even though I was a new troop leader fresh out of Royal Military College, I got along with my troop pretty well. My senior NCOs had all spent long years in Germany, and had no great love for officers. They would often regale me with stories of previous troop leaders, squadron commanders and commanding officers who all seemed like idiots. Sometimes their stories became so outrageous, I was convinced they were trying to get a rise out of me, or to see what they could get me to believe. I took the stories in stride, told some of my own about officers and NCOs alike, and could usually get a laugh out of them too. In the end, they seemed to appreciate that I was diligent without being difficult, and more or less knew when to get out of the way and let them do their part of the business.

I could tell that they liked me well enough when we were in Arkansas doing work-up training to deploy to Bosnia with the 3rd Battalion, Royal Canadian Regiment (RCR) Battle Group. It was my birthday during the exercise, and that evening in the troop hide they gathered together and surprised me with gifts. First was a lawn chair that they had salvaged from a garbage heap and repaired with green duct tape. They passed it up to me in the turret of my Cougar, and I set it up on the front deck so that I could sit in it with my feet on the gun barrel. Next was a cigar of unknown origin or quality, which I lit. I was sure that I cut a fine figure, sitting on my lawn chair with my feet up smoking a cigar, as the troop were all smiling at me, their eyes shining.

It was then that they passed up my final gift, which the troop warrant explained, was a cake. This must have taken some effort, I thought, and I felt suddenly moved. As I thought of some suitable words to say, the troop warrant placed the cake on the front deck of my vehicle. As soon as he did, the entire troop turned around as one and ran away.

One of the most hated items in our ration packs at that time was the baked cherry dessert, which resembled nothing more than a foil bag full of plastic dog vomit. It was one of these "cakes" that the troop had given me., but the reason that they ran was that pushed through the centre of it was a lit "thunder flash" pyrotechnic. I fell off the Cougar trying to get away from it, breaking my chair and losing my cigar. It went off with a crack, spreading dog vomit and cherries all over the front of my vehicle, and spreading a thin paste over the episcopes that had to be scrubbed off. The troop left me to explain to the Squadron Commander on the radio what the noise was about, gathered in small groups around me laughing hysterically. As I said, they liked me.

Our tour in Bosnia was many things: long, busy, boring, exciting, hot, and cold. We hustled to execute operations that often amounted to long standing observation posts over empty roads or buildings, mounted from within our frigid vehicles or from burned out buildings where we squatted. We escorted the movement of factional weapons, took stock of weapons at cantonment sites, built and confirmed targeting lists to quickly stop hostilities, searched buildings, cars and people for weapons and contraband, and tried to put a dent in both the heroin and illegal logging trades. We also drank a lot of local coffee, got into car accidents with every description of Eastern European car you've never heard of, and bought bootleg CDs by the thousand. Our interactions with the various military forces whose fighting we were meant to curtail were always hostile, stopping just short of violence.

Near the end of our tour, when the Officer Commanding (OC) the Squadron gathered all the troop leaders and the Squadron Sergeant Major together one evening to brief us on a new mission, I'd be lying if I said there was much enthusiasm.

"This one is different," he said. "We're going to change an international border."

This caught my interest, and I knew immediately where we were going to do this.

In our patrolling of the massive area of operations, we had found a very picturesque little village called Martin Brod. It was a farming community nestled against the Croatian border with a beautiful set of waterfalls just behind it.

We had set up camp there for weeks on end, befriending a monk who lived in a local chapel and who spoke passable German. He showed us where a massive minefield was located within the town. In a stroke of genius, we had the engineers clear a path into the centre of the minefield, and space for us to park, creating probably the strongest defensive position in 3 RCR for our home.

The Una River ran through the village, and the bridge across it had been seized by the Croatian forces during the war, moving the border to that point from where it had been originally, along a ridgeline 500 metres further west. This small change made a huge difference to the Bosnians living in Martin Brod – it separated most of the farmers from their fields, as they could not cross through the border.

The OC gave us only the sparest details of the plan, without a location even. At that point all I knew was that it was called "Operation Shannon," allegedly after some commanding general's driver/mistress. It was all top secret, to keep the Croatians in the dark, but I wasn't that surprised when I left the briefing to be accosted by one of our interpreters.

"When are we going to Martin Brod?" she asked.

"What do you mean?" I stammered.

"For the big mission?" she asked.

Within hours it was clear that the operation was not secret at all, and that everyone from the camp cleaners to their intelligence handlers knew about it. We were soon called into another meeting, this time with the interpreters as well, where the OC made it clear that the thing that we had previously talked about was cancelled. He could give no further details, but the interpreters gave each other knowing winks.

Things, however, were not so simple. A few weeks later the OC arranged for all three troop leaders to meet one afternoon at the platoon house just south of Bosanski Petrovac, known to everyone simply as "Bos P." An isolated building made largely out of plywood, it had no local nationals working in it at all. While there, he briefed us on the plan – Operation Shannon was back on, and the target was Martin Brod.

The Croatian border guards at the bridge lived in a small building near the river. There were half a dozen of them, armed with Kalashnikovs and pistols and an RPG. The real concern, however, was further away. The closest Croatian military unit that could respond to a "NATO invasion" was an M-84 squadron (the Yugoslavian variant of the T-72). That caused some concerned looks, as the Cougar's 76mm gun and light armour was no match for a main battle tank.

The plan was for most of the Battle Group to piquet the various local military forces who might respond negatively to the operation or take advantage of it to seize territory of their own. One of the recce troops was held in the east of the AO watching the Serbs. The second troop, with TOW-Under-Armour vehicles attached was to be positioned to overlook the town in case the M-84s showed up. And my troop was to seize the crossing and re-establish it 500 m west.

To accomplish this, I was given more assets than I had ever had. A platoon of infantry in Grizzlies was attached to me, along with a section of engineers and two HLVWs carrying car wrecks to create obstacles at the new border. I was the camp's alternate Forward Air Controller, and I had communications with a PC-3 Orion who would monitor for any radio signals from the M-84s that would suggest they were moving, and there was close air support being flown out of Italy if required. More ominously, we were also given an armoured ambulance – to signal our serious intent, or so it was explained to me.

There was only one part of the plan that was dictated to me that I didn't like. In doctrinally correct fashion, my troop was to take the bridge from both sides at once. What this meant was that one of my patrols had to cross into Croatia early on, and take a very long route to reach the bridge at the same time as the rest of us. I was worried that they would get stopped by the Croatians, or tip our hand, or get lost or stuck en route – in essence, there was too much risk for not enough gain. I favoured relying on speed and surprise. The discussion about this point got heated as I stood my ground, but in the end, I had no choice but to say "yes, sir" and sit in red faced silence.

When I briefed my own troop, they were worried about two things – the lone patrol moving through Croatia, and the M-84s. There was little that could be done about the first issue, and so the conversation focused on the second. We knew the ground around the village well, and it was not ideal for the TUA. The switchbacks were heavily wooded, and any fighting was going to be done at point blank range. We would have to fire and jockey around a corner or otherwise find cover before they returned fire. After studying what details we had on the M-84, we decided that there were only two weak points that our gun could penetrate – either at the seam between the turret and the hull, or straight through the gap in the armour for the gunner's sight. We couldn't come up with anything better than that.

"Just like ol' Luke ramming one down the thermal exhaust port," said my troop sergeant, grinning.

There was no date fixed for the operation, but we were all summoned again to convene in Bos P for a back brief to the Battle Group Commander. Every one of the junior commanders, such as myself, were to brief the details of their part of the plan to the Colonel. The platoon house was packed to the rafters with nearly every officer in the Battle Group seated on rough benches facing a map board and an enlarged aerial image of the town. The CO started off the briefing with some words of encouragement, and then we began to cycle through the commanders of each part of the plan.

When it came to my part, I stood up and looked at the CO, then paused.

I'm not sure exactly what came over me, or why I thought I'd get away with it, but as I briefed the actions by my troop and all the attachments, I briefed my preferred plan – assaulting the bridge from one end – rather than the OC's plan of sending a patrol the long way around. As I was speaking, I tried not to look at the OC and Battle Captain (BC), who were sitting beside each other deep in the audience, each turning progressively redder in the face. I could see that the OC was going to launch himself off of the bench to correct me as soon as I paused for breath, so kept going. As I brought my briefing to an end, the Battle Group CO spoke first:

"I like it. This sounds good."

The OC sank back into his seat, his face turning from red to a mottled purple.

When the briefing was over, I could barely look the OC in the eye. He didn't say anything to me, but the BC leaned in and whispered in my ear:

"Your fucking plan better work."

Thankfully, I was confident that it would.

H-hour was set for 0300 hours on Christmas Eve. Before we left camp, my Troop Warrant dragged me between the weatherhaven shelters where we lived, and held out a bottle of "Head and Shoulders" shampoo. I opened the bottle cautiously and gave it a smell – whiskey.

"My wife sends them to me in care packages," he said.

I took a swig and handed it back for him to do the same. "Break a leg," he said.

Just before we rolled out of camp for the hundred-kilometre drive to Martin Brod, I received one last change to the plan. I was to pick up a combat photographer at a grid reference in the middle of nowhere. How he got there, and why I needed him, no one knew. I added the location to my map, and we rolled away.

The majority of the trip was wet and cold but uneventful. I sipped at a massive thermal cup of coffee that I had filled up in the mess in Camp Maple Leaf. I didn't think much about the combat photographer that we had to pick up until we reached the location.

Parked by the side of the road was a black SUV with a winch on the front bumper and German license plates. No one in the Battle Group drove a car with anything but DND plates. I hopped down to meet the photographer, who got out of the driver's seat when we approached. He was dressed in the uniform of an RCR Sergeant Major, but I had never met him before. His hair touched his ears, he had a non-standard pistol in a non-standard holster on his hip, and unlike the rest of us who wore issued boots, his were some special kind of footwear that stood out like a sore thumb. There was not a camera in sight anywhere, and there wasn't a Sergeant Major in the RCR who would get caught dead looking like this guy did.

He must have seen my look because he launched right into his pitch. "I'm from a special unit with expertise in urban ops, and I'm coming with you to take control of the mission if needed to achieve success."

I'd already had a few bad experiences with the "special" troops operating in our area before, and I saw red as soon as I heard him say "take control." The irony of my reaction, compared to that of my OC at the back brief, is not lost on me now, but I didn't see it all those years ago. I won't repeat what I said to the "combat photographer," but we left him on the side of the road and carried on.

We approached the village from the north along a narrow road that skirted the river. Our wheels on one side felt like they were in danger of sliding into the water, while those on the other brushed against the rock wall from which the road was carved. It was a long slow drive along that route, without headlights. We paused for about fifteen minutes when we were still a good distance from Martin Brod, so that we could hit h-hour precisely. When we rolled for the final approach, I hit play on the Walkman wired into our intercom system, playing some punk rock that I thought would be the right soundtrack for the operation. My gunner, who preferred classical, grimaced a little at the noise in his headset.

As planned, the troop raced through the village with my vehicle in the lead. I popped my head up to confirm that no obstacle had been dragged across the bridge as we crashed through the wooden barriers at the border. The building where the Croats slept was pitch black.

The plan was to drive right up to it and exploit surprise, but I told the driver to "halt" too late and the vehicle slid on the ice and hit the side of the building with a crash that must have shook them inside like an earth quake. Within seconds, it seemed, a half dozen Croats came piling out of the front door, all armed and half-dressed and angry.

I looked behind me, and the rest of the troop had become hung up on the wreckage on the bridge and were stalled. I thought about depressing the coaxial machinegun to at least point it at the Croats, but with the height of the vehicle and the slope of the ground, it was pointing uselessly over their heads. I suppose I could have buttoned up and waited for the infantry, but with "Bad

Religion" screaming in my headset, I did something else.

I popped out of my hatch to stand on top of the turret, pistol out, and started shouting at the Croats to drop their weapons. Body armour was too bulky to wear in the turret, and our headsets didn't fit over ballistic helmets, so I was in greasy coveralls and a crew helmet liner with my callsign written on the front with a big black marker. Though I don't think I cut a very imposing figure, by the time the infantry arrived I had disarmed all the Croats and they were lined up against the wall. The first phase of what we later called "The Battle of the Brod" had taken about thirty seconds from the point we (accidently) rammed the building.

There was no mechanism to keep the Croats as prisoners, and so they were restrained and herded into the back of the Squadron Liaison Officer's vehicle. We wanted to take some of the sting out of being captured in their own country, and so planned to take their flag down from the pole and give it to them to take with them, but by this point it had disappeared. Eventually, the infantry platoon warrant admitted to having kept it, and once returned to the Croats, they were driven deeper into the country and dropped off at a deserted crossroads from where they could walk into the nearest town.

We spent the rest of the morning and the next day on the high ground that was now the international border, waiting nervously for any sign of the M-84s. The Croatians didn't send tanks, but they did send dismounted infantry to probe our positions, which was a more difficult threat for us to deal with. My quick-thinking NCOs found a solution that keep them at a safe distance without escalating the situation into combat – the used the Cougar's searchlight, which was incredibly powerful, to expose them as they tried to reach us. Every time they were caught in our beams they turned around, and by the time it was daylight, they stopped trying.

We were disappointed to learn that the Battle Group could not convince the Bosnian border guards to occupy the new border we had established, for fear of attack by the Croatians, and so we were forced to do it for them. We built up the obstacles at that point in the road, suing car wrecks and whatever else we could find, so that we would be ready to hold the position overnight again. It took the entire troop to secure the position and do the necessary work, which meant that there was no rest for anyone.

By that night, we started rotating crews off the position, just in time for the Squadron Sergeant Major to bring up a hot haybox meal of turkey and all the fixings. Over dinner, it was decided that the officers and senior NCOs would take all the sentry shifts that night, Christmas Eve, and so with a bellyful of turkey I found myself on sentry for four hours on one of the coldest nights I could remember, By the time I was done, I had been up for nearly 48 hours, and fell asleep without quite managing to get undressed.

When I woke up the next day, I found a reminder that it was Christmas morning. Sitting on the foot of my cot was a gift from my troop. It was a small cardboard box from our ration packs with a bright red ribbon drawn on it with a staedler marker.

Scrawled on the back of the box was a note:

"Your plan worked - so no candle this time."

And inside was a baked cherry dessert. As I said, they liked me well enough.

Warrant Officer Duncan Nyberg

Duncan Nyberg joined the Regiment in 1994. He was deployed to Kosovo as a member of Admin Troop within the Royal Canadian Dragoon Reconnaissance Squadron. In his civilian career, he is an elevator mechanic with the International Union of Elevator Constructors, Local 50.

I was one of four Rangers that went on the tour to Kosovo in 1999: there were supposed to be five of us, but one got cut at the last minute. We all took rank reductions from Master Corporal or Sergeant to Corporal to get on the tour, and got incorporated into Recce Squadron of the RCD (Royal Canadian Dragoons) which was part of the RCR (Royal Canadian Regiment) battle group.

Reservists weren't popular on this deployment: the RCD was forced to take us, and they didn't want to. The Army finally told them they had to take 20% reservists, and in the end, they only took 15%. The reason was, they had a full squadron – all the guys they needed to fill their positions, so every reservist they took on tour was one less Dragoon who got to go. So, they didn't want us along, and they took every chance to remind us.

This was a full-up recce squadron: four troops, an assault troop, and a full echelon – there were more than 200 guys in that squadron. So naturally, they put all the reservists in Admin Troop: I was an HLVW driver, and my job was to drive the fuel pod truck. It was all right once we got over there, and every now and then we got attached to one of the recce troops when guys went on their home leave.

By the time we got there, which was in November 1999, all of the shooting and bombing was pretty much over and done with. The Serbs had been pushed out after the NATO bombing campaign and had basically gotten right out of Dodge, but they were still just over the border between Kosovo and Serbia.

But there were still about 15% of the population in Kosovo that were Serbian, and there were a lot of worries that they would be targeted by the Albanians, the Albanian Kosovars. So, we were basically there to protect the local Serbs, and to keep the Serbs and the Kosovars from killing each other.

Our Camp was called CAMP DK (short for Donja Koretica), not far from the city of Pristina, the capital of Kosovo.

What I remember most about it was the smell: the whole country smelled like burning wood, grass and a hint of burning plastic.

The terrain was very hilly and green, with lots of grass and small farms, but not very many trees. Apparently, the local population was always cutting down trees to use for firewood, so wood was scarce! Small farmhouses were everywhere, with clay tiled roofs: when they had roofs. Over half of them were either burnt out or had damaged or collapsed roofs, covered over with blue tarps to protect them from the elements, a lot of them with the UN or UNHCR logo on them.

I was given the impression that lots of damage was made by retreating Serbs once our forces pushed them out. But the Albanian Kosovars were generally hospitable towards us and friendly, they were always calling us: "My friend my friend."

There were hundreds of dogs roaming the countryside. Apparently, when the Albanians fled they just freed their family dogs because they didn't have time or the means to take them with them. It wasn't uncommon to see packs of 20 or 30 running through the fields.

So right around the end of December, I got sent out to 2 Troop to be a surveillance operator – the GIB (Guy in Back), which means I got all the shit jobs.

We were out patrolling the border between Kosovo and Serbia – although really, Kosovo was still a province of Serbia – and we were patrolling overtly, with our lights on, being visibly present. We wanted both sides, the Serbs and the Albanians, to know we were there.

We were patrolling around the area of Podujevo, in northeast Kosovo, on New Year's Eve. Everyone had been talking about Y2K; how it was going to crash all the computers or be the end of the world, and there I was on duty for Y2K on a hilltop in Kosovo.

There was a blizzard on, about two feet of snow had already fallen and more was coming down. There was always a dismounted sentry when we were in an OP (Observation Post), and because I was the reservist on the crew, guess who got that job? To make it even better, the snow was coming down so fast I had to shovel to keep the Coyote from getting buried in a snowdrift.

So, there I was on New Year's Eve, shoveling snow in the dark, with my radio headset on listening to the means. And just before midnight, everyone comes on the radio to say Happy New Year, or shout at each other, or whatever: there were even a couple of Brits singing over the radio. It was a five or 10 minutes of complete uncontrolled, crazy radio traffic.

I'm listening to all this, and shoveling away, when all of a sudden bullets start flying overhead. I dive onto the ground, which is really into a snowbank and I'm trying to raise someone on the radio to give a contact report. Only I can't, because there's too many people singing or saying happy new years to each other, and meanwhile we're in the middle of a crossfire.

There was a Serbian border post just on their side of the border, and an Albanian or a Kosovar post on their side. It turned out later what had happened was the Serbs had decided to celebrate the New Year by getting drunk and right at midnight firing their rifles up into the air.

The Albanians thought they were shooting at them, so they started firing back. And of course, we were right in the middle.

Eventually, it died down – probably after both sides ran out of ammunition – but for a while there I was on my belly in a snowbank thinking: "Happy Y2K to you too."

Domestic Operations

The Canadian Armed Forces have a long history of conducting operations in support of civil powers within Canada. Whether in response to security issues (FLQ Crisis, Oka Crisis), air disasters (Swissair Flight 111), flooding (Red River and others), forest fires (in Ontario and BC), or in support of major events (1976 and 2010 Olympics, G8/20 Summits in 2002 and 2010), a key part of the Canadian Forces mandate is to be ready to have a positive impact "at home."

Lieutenant Mark Benfield

Mark Benfield joined the Rangers as a Private in 1975, commissioning in 1977. He served on Operation GAMESCAN from May 1976 to August 1976. In his civilian career, he is a Professor in the Department of Oceanography and Coastal Sciences at Louisiana State University.

The 1976 Olympics were the first and only time that I carried a loaded weapon operationally as a Ranger. I was a trooper and was posted to the 8th Canadian Hussars where I was attached to A Squadron. As far as I know, I was the only Ranger to be deployed on security duty at the Games (known as Operation GAMESCAN) and certainly one of the few reservists. After finishing my High School final exams early, I took flew "Pem Air" to Pembroke in May and reported to the 8CH. I was the only reservist in the squadron and most of my fellow Hussars were only privates. I also had my 404 (military drivers licence).

We spent a lot of time training. Many hours on the range working with the FNC1A1, SMG and 9mm pistol. We also learned how to fire riot guns using various CS canisters. Much of the curriculum involved riot control and we took turns being soldiers or protesters. The latter was a lot more fun and it was informative to see how easy it was to provoke one's friends to anger in the heat (literally and figuratively) of the moment. Many films and lectures were devoted to learning mob psychology and how protests were coordinated by agitators controlling the mob from the rear.

We finally deployed to Montreal where we were billeted at Marymount High School, our home away from home for several weeks prior to and a week following the games. It was a great place. We had a bar downstairs with a jukebox, pinball machines, a pool table, and table tennis. Discipline was strict and we lived in fear of running afoul of Sergeant-Major Elliot and his knobby pace stick that he was always threatening to insert in places normally reserved for colonoscopies. My troop and I became a close-knit team. I was fortunate to serve under some outstanding junior NCOs – Master Corporal Steeves and Corporal Brown. There was no Reg Force/Reserve distinction. We were all there to do a serious job.

Our primary task was to guard the athletes at their training sites and we were all pumped up and ready to defend the Olympians from any terror attack. To put some context on the security situation, the 1972 Munich Olympics were the site of the Munich Massacre by Palestinian terrorists. One would have thought that we'd be heavily armed. The reality was, we were given just five rounds of ammunition. At the training sites, we were generally issued 9mm Browning pistols. What value our meager ammunition would have been in the event that Carlos the Jackal et al had shown up was questionable. Not only that, but our rules of engagement required us to state in both official languages: HALT! HALT HANDS UP! HALT OR I'LL FIRE. HALT I'M PREPARING TO FIRE! Needless to say, we practiced those phrases in a rapid staccato and HALT! HALT HAUT LES MAINS! HALT OU JE TIR! HALT JE SUIS PRET A TIRER! still roll effortlessly off my tongue.

I came to regret having my military licence because on some days, my troop leader, Lt. Leduc needed a driver and I was the only one in the troop who could drive a jeep. Montreal traffic and its psychotic drivers were terrifying. The bad brakes on the jeep didn't help much either. Still, it was a change of pace and a chance to get away from the busy work that often befell anyone off duty back at Marymount. A few years later I ran into Lt. Leduc in Gagetown during RESO Phase I & II. He confessed to being equally terrified by Montreal traffic.

There were different levels of security passes and we had to wear ours at all times. For security troops, our passes were the highest level and they enabled us to enjoy the games on our off-duty time from a remarkable perspective. I was able to walk on the sidelines of the Olympic Stadium and watch track and field events from a fantastic vantage point. I saw Olympic boxing near ringside. Our passes also got us into some primo bars that were reserved the various national teams. I have no idea who invited us, but several members of my troop and I wound up drinking 16 oz cans of Swiss lager followed by schnapps chasers at the Swiss Lounge as guests of their soccer team. Sadly, the team and their coach were drowning their sorrows because they'd been removed from competition as punishment for defying the apartheid sports embargo and playing a game against South Africa prior to the games. We were all best of friends by the end of the night and that's about all I recall of the evening!

One bizarre aspect of the games was the attitude of the press towards the soldiers. They generally hated us and took any opportunity to portray the forces in a negative light. One night they hired hookers to proposition the sentries patrolling outside our high school base. Another occasion I recall vividly. I was deployed on anti-sniper duty on a rooftop overlooking a field where they were rehearsing for the closing ceremonies. I had an FN and binoculars. It was a hot day and in front of me was a field of young women dressed in shorts and halter-tops going through their dance moves. Unfortunately, below me was a film crew with their cameras aimed directly at me, hoping to film me scoping out the young ladies in the field. Sadly, for them (and for me), I was the most diligent anti-sniper of Operation GAMESCAN for the three hours I was on that rooftop!

All good things come to an end. When I look back on my time in the Queen's

York Rangers, Operation GAMESCAN was one of the two highlights of my military career. The other, also with the 8CH was when I commanded the RHQ Recce Troop during RV85. There is something about the responsibility of carrying live ammunition in the wake of Munich that made our tasking crystal clear. The lives of innocent athletes were very much in our hands. For this young Canadian soldier, it was an awesome responsibility.

War in Afghanistan

Canada's longest war, running from 2001 to 2014, this was also Canada's first sustained combat operation since the Korean War. More than 40,000 Canadian Armed Forces members serves during the campaign, in which 158 soldiers and 7 civilians lost their lives.

Sergeant Matthew Wood

Matthew Wood served with the Queen's York Rangers from 2002 to 2019 and was employed as a patrol commander and troop warrant officer. He deployed to Afghanistan in 2006 and participated in Operation Medusa as a member of the psychological operations team. He is currently a police officer with the Toronto Police Service.

When I was twenty one years old, I was halfway around the world. Following the conclusion of Operation Medusa, our convoy was headed back to Kandahar Airfield (KAF) from Forward Operating Base Ma'Sum Ghar. The trip started out with a little excitement. While the vehicles mustered for the long journey home, a fighter jet suddenly dashed overhead. For a brief moment I thought yet another rocket had been fired at us. This had become the norm. But the convoy rolled ahead, business as usual, snaking its way through the chicane and out onto one of the rare paved roads that led towards the city. Route Hyena (of Paul Gross fame) had not yet been built.

A few minutes into the trip back, the convoy slowed and ultimately came to a stop. There was some unknown trouble up ahead. Traffic congestion, mechanical failure, a security threat, I wasn't sure. What I was sure of was that I didn't like the idea of being static, especially alongside a series of tanker trucks. The Afghan National Police (ANP) officer manning the check point up ahead did little to ease the tension.

The convoy lurched forward once again. As was standard operating procedure, the lead call sign called out suspicious vehicles along the route, indicating whether the driver was alone, of fighting age, or if the vehicle seemed weighed down (possibly with explosives). The convoy shifted from left to right, or right to left in order to create standoff between itself and the potential threat.

We rounded a corner, making a right turn onto the main highway that would take us into Kandahar city. This turn was all too familiar as we'd made this trip several times in the few months that we'd been in theatre. As we began to pick up speed, a flash of white-orange filled my windshield. We'd missed a motorcycle in the ditch. A fireball worthy of a Michael Bay movie instantly engulfed the up-armoured G-Wagen just ahead of me. "Push, push, push!" was the message that came through the radio. I thought to myself "just don't stop in the kill zone".

As the crippled G-Wagen drifted to the right, I manoeuvred my truck through the flames and around the wreck only to find that the convoy had come to a stop. Jay and Pete appeared outside my passenger-side door, banging, trying to get it. It was theirs that had been hit, and they were both okay. A relief.

Instructions came quickly to stop and establish a cordon. The G-Wagen was immobilized and we would hold our position.

Dave and I dismounted, pushed out, and formed a perimeter in unison with crews from the rest of the convoy. I stood on the driver's side of the road which was now littered with fleshy bits, motorcycle parts, and a pair of dead donkeys. Looking up at a four-storey apartment complex, I scanned each window for threats. The building seemed to be growing taller with each minute that passed. The ground level featured a number of small storefronts, most of which had hurriedly closed up following the blast. I couldn't possibly keep an eye on all at once. "An attack always follows an ambush", I thought.

As I dutifully completed my fives-and-twenties, a man appeared from around the right side of the building and walked quickly in my direction. "Get the fuck back!" was my response. A message he quickly understood. Although our team had been assigned a permanent interpreter, this had been the first day that he had called in sick. Coincidence? The same man came back a few short seconds later, this time keeping his distance, beckoning me to come with him. I leveled my C7 to reinforce the message. Again, he understood. It wasn't until a few minutes later that I, in turn, understood his message.

The man returned again, only this time he was carrying the limp body of a young boy. His message was clear. I shouted up to Kris, who was manning the turret-mounted "6", and asked for him to call for the medic. It was clear that the boy was in rough shape. His white jammies were soaked in red. The source was a wound to his head. Shrapnel from the blast must have caught him, partially scalping him in the process. But the wound wasn't bleeding. Had it been cauterized? Something seemed off.

The boy was conscious and breathing but wasn't crying. That amount of blood had to have come from somewhere. I did my best to cover the head wound with my field dressing (hardly an adequate first aid treatment) but needed to figure out where the other wound was.

I began an extensive search of the boy's body. Arms: fine. Chest: fine. Back: fine. Legs: fine. There was only one place left to look. I pulled the boys pants down and exposed the source. There was a baseball-sized cavity immediately adjacent to his genitals. Oddly enough, I couldn't help but think how lucky the kid was. The important parts were still intact. I did what little I could to reassure him.

I ran back to check on the medic, only to learn that he was at the rear of the convoy, preferring not to cross to our end due to the hazard posed by the burning truck. It wasn't until this moment that I realized that there were still live rockets, grenades, and ammunition inside. Every few seconds the crackle of 5.56 could be heard from inside. Pete, Jay, and Dave were shuttling back and forth as best they could to pull the explosives (among other things) out of the fire. For this, four soldiers would be awarded the medal for bravery, only two of whom were truly deserving. Dave would be overlooked. A shame really. They forgot the Kraft Dinner.

After a few minutes' work, I convinced the medic that his services were required. He quickly realized that the boy needed a medevac. A scrap of paper I wrote on at the time reminds me that: the boy was 12 years old; he had an open skull fracture with penetration to the right of his head; he had a wound to the left pelvis which had not gone all the way through; the bleeding was controlled; he had a blood pressure of 94 over 50; he had a heart rate of 90 beats per minute; and that he had a respiratory rate of 22 breaths per minute.

I went in search of the convoy commander to relay the information, only to find that a young, seemingly-untried master corporal was at the helm. After some convincing, the message was relayed. It was then that I realized that the local fire department had arrived. I watched in awe as the crew, in their contrasting jammies and hard hats, pulled the hose from their circa-1950 fire truck. The wreck was now burning at a temperature so hot that the bullet-proof glass had melted. I wondered just how much of the ammunition the guys had been able to recover. The steady crackle and pop were a clue.

As the fire crew inched closer to the blaze, a sudden explosion knocked the lot of them to the ground. The myriad of holes that appeared in the firehose indicated that it was a grenade that had just cooked off. Before I could picture just how badly the crew had been hurt, to my amazement, they sprung back to their feet and continued fighting the fire (albeit with a far less effective sprinkler-hose).

Turning back to the convoy commander, I found that the request for a medevac had been denied. I learned that the suicide bomber had not acted alone. A coordinated attack struck two other convoys, and those attacks had resulted in Canadian casualties. Corporal Robert Mitchell and Sergeant Craig Gillam both died that day. Pete had been our only Canadian casualty, sustaining a second degree burn to his left arm. The blast had penetrated a gap in the G-Wagen's armour (a souvenir from a past tour) and Pete got a taste. We were instructed to wait for recovery, and then press on back to base.

With the boy still in need of medical attention, I began looking around for options. I noticed that the ANP had established an exterior perimeter beyond our own perimeter to keep all the civilian vehicles back. It was then that I saw the distinct red and white colours of an ambulance. I grabbed Brady, who was nearby, and jogged about 200 meters down the line of halted armoured vehicles towards the ambulance. I did my best to gesture that they were required, though I had never really played charades much. The driver seemed to get the message, and promptly drove down to meet the boy, leaving me and Brady behind. We jogged the 200 meters back and I damn near keeled over from the combination of heat, weight, exhaustion, dehydration, and exertion. I have a distinct memory of everything fading to black and thinking to myself: "if we come under attack now, I'm toast." I have since developed an appreciation for cardio training.

In the following hours, the boy would get ushered to the hospital in the truck (which, as it turned out, wasn't actually an ambulance); the wreckage would get loaded onto a flatbed (that I only recently discovered had been driven by my friend Jon, a former Ranger himself); and we would make it back safely to base.

This is just one of the stories from the six months we spent overseas.

At the age of 21, I dropped out of college and volunteered for the mission in Afghanistan. I had the opportunity to experience something that few have, or will ever experience. I am thankful each day that my team made it back (almost) in one piece, and I am eternally grateful for the sacrifices made by those who didn't.

Our battle group was later awarded the Commander-in-Chief Unit Commendation with a citation that reads:

During August and September 2006, the 1st Battalion, The Royal Canadian Regiment Battle Group played a decisive role in one of the largest ground combat operations in the history of NATO. Deployed to an area of Afghanistan with fierce enemy resistance and extremely difficult terrain, the members of the battle group resolutely defeated a well-coordinated insurgent force in the area surrounding Kandahar City.

Succeeding where larger forces had failed, they prevented the enemy from realizing their goals of capturing the city and weakening international resolve and cohesion.

It's hard to believe that it was so long ago today that I was standing on the side of that highway, watching that G-Wagen burn, and thinking of what could have been.

What a trip.

Master Corporal James Balancio

James Balancio joined the Queen's York Rangers in 1997. He served 2 tours in Kandahar, Afghanistan between 2006 to 2009. In his civilian career, he is an Armed Nuclear Security Officer at Ontario Power Generation.

It's February 2009. We saunter through a village that appears untouched by our foot patrols for many, many months. The villagers are more curious than anti coalition. The village men stand in knots with toothy smiles as their children flock us for candy. All women are customarily hidden. The pattern of life appears normal.

A motorcycle putts its way through the main alley. Our search of the vehicle is quick and routine before it moves on and stops at pod of men gathered by the gate of a family compound.

The driver is in his twenties—fighting age—with the telltale leather vest over pajamas, capped with a turban in the Pashtun way, and a chin-strap beard. There are smiles and chatter about the day. There are smiles and chatter about our patrol. The motorcycle drives off casually.

"Probably telling them there's trouble coming," says Jasher about the motorcyclist.

An old man steps forth, smiles some more, and gently shepherds the children away from us as we prepare to move on. He is dark with leathery skin under a white beard, and on another day, I might talk to this elder, for he appears to be in charge. The children cackle and laugh, but his gentle whispers are heard over their noise, and they scurry away.

The pastel colours of children's' clothing disappear into family compounds. The alleys of the village are deserted within calm seconds. The pattern of life goes from normal to nil. We take note of this painfully obvious sign, but figure we have some time.

Our mixed platoon moves just a few meters...

Snap-snap! Snap-snap-snap!

Crack-crack! Crack-crack-crack!

My mind and body enter fight mode. The hamster in my head runs frantically inside his wheel.

Our mixed platoon is brought to an abrupt halt by the sound of bullets slapping against surrounding mud walls.

We slowly take a knee. The urge to dive flat is negated by the weight on our backs. It's late in our tour and by now everyone knows that going prone with a heavy pack means never coming up again. Being immobile is a sin to our instincts.

Heads pivot and turn in all directions. The sounds are echoing from all directions. "Where is it?!" yells the Sniper Sergeant. No one answers him, because no one knows. I flick off my safety. I wait for a chance to get violent, suspecting every corner and bush I can process.

"Back up, back up!" I say to The Team behind me after a very sudden revelation. The surrounding mud walls form an alley with all of us lined up in it, one after the other, and the gunfire appears to be up ahead. I imagine an insurgent with a PKM machine gun blazing hot fire down the alley at us. We're such juicy targets that we might as well be lined up inside the barrel of his gun. "Back up, back up!"

We scurry back inch by inch with great difficulty on our knees. I back into Jasher's skinny form, and with an assuring hand on my shoulder he says, "Hold on, I think they're withdrawing." Jasher always sees things before I do.

The insurgent volley becomes half-hearted and scattered and fades to nothing. The only gunfire comes from the friendlies ahead of us. Our friendlies up front are probably striking at empty grape rows by now, slapping dirt to no avail. Then everything stops.

My mind and body exit fight-mode and re-enters the world. I slowly begin to hear wind whisper through the alleys of this village. I can hear the sounds of nagging women, playing children, and dishes - of all things, dishes - being washed under running water through the window of someone's home. These villagers are accustomed to gunfire.

"What the hell was that?" asks Brody, referring to the scant gun play. Brody is a recent addition to The Team from another district bereft of gunfights. His world before walking with us is about convoys and roadside I-E-D's. This is his first random walk with an isolated and hastily formed group in the "back forty" of Kandahar.

"That," says Jasher, "was a shoot 'n scoot. A couple of them hit us with a light load, and then they run. They're trying to dummy us into an ambush. Dangerous as fuck."

"Fair enough," says Brody, "what do we do then?"

"We sit and wait. The other platoons are all around us in a half-kilometer radius. Let's not hit them."

The Officer signals with the bottom of a clenched fist toward us. Hold Firm. Then he makes a slow, sideways chop at waist level. Deploy and go to ground. The signals are pantomimed down the line. The mixed platoon is here to stay.

We shuffle into our spots without a word, being mindful that all arcs of a circle around us must be covered by our eyes and guns. We move methodically, carefully selecting folds in the ground that offer protection, proper fields of view, and most importantly, comfort.

I'm not infantry by trade, but I know this: An infantryman's journey is to search for comfort through adversity as it is a spiritual man's journey to search for himself through God.

I get lucky. My spot is behind a low grape-row with small bushes that hide me somewhat, but I can see out to a couple of hundred meters. The soil of the grape-row appears sufficient enough to stop bullets. A brick wall or a flight out of Kandahar would be better protection, but I have no time for that. The best part is the grape-row behind me offers a nice gradient for me to plant my butt and lean my pack against. The weight shifts from my feet to the grape-row, and I'm truly happy.

I look left and right to check on the Team. This is my first month as Team Leader, and I promise myself to always check on them. Jasher finds a similar spot to my left. Good. Habib the Terp settles in beside me. Brody finds the corner of a mud wall to my right and gives me thumbs up.

I look around and find all arcs are covered by the rest of the mixed platoon. There are no gaps in our circle. The Officer takes a central position with his radio and consults a map. His calm tells me we're all where we're supposed to be. Fifteen shooters sit ready.

Jasher and I nod at each other and smirk. Here we go again.

After a few minutes of silence, I relax my grip on my rifle and light a cigarette. Jasher shoves some chew into his lower lip from a hockey puck of tobacco. His light machine gun sits on its bipod legs like a stalking leopard. Habib tears into a ration pack almost with his nose.

Brody gives us a confused stare. He's wondering why we seem to be slacking. I smile as I tap my watch and point at the earth below me. We're gonna be here a while, get comfy. Brody nods and settles into his spot by shoving his feet out forward from under him.

The village remains silent, save for the muffled sounds of children in their homes.

Snap-snap! Snap-snap-snap!

Crack-crack! Crack-crack-crack!

It's three cigarettes later. Army Math: 45 to 60 minutes since settling in.

The enemy offers another shoot 'n scoot before he disappears again. I can't read his mind, but I'm sure he's surprised our mixed platoon didn't move, so attempts another obvious bait. The Officer plans on this, having used ourselves as counter-bait. The Officer is telling the enemy, "we saw your bait; will you fall for ours?"

The enemy doesn't fall for it. He doesn't manoeuvre his elements to surround us. He waits in his own unseen kill zones, and a stalemate of wits ensues for a while.

The powers above decide to break off the stalemate and order a redeployment of all platoons. They decide that waiting means the enemy will strengthen their position with more reinforcements or more elaborate traps, and our Highers are right. The enemy has a tendency to be more devilish with time. So, we're ordered to move and see if the enemy will do the same or make a mistake.

An American Captain, some hundreds of meters away from us, suggests pummeling the ground in the direction of the enemy with smoke shells from a distant battery of big guns. The American Captain's plan is to help all the platoons to redeploy under the cover of a wall of grey smoke. This is common practice, so we wait for the smoke cover.

"Golf-Two-One, this is Warrior-Six, Fire Mission, over!" he says with his American twang on the 'net. A Fire Mission is the radio call to bring the big guns to action. Somewhere, about fifteen kilometers away from us, a detachment of gunners is being kicked out of their cots and hurried to their guns.

The reply comes in a rapid monotone that sounds like a computer streaming data, "Warrior-Six-this-is-Golf-Two-One-send-Fire-Mission-over."

"Golf-Two-One, Fire Mission! Grid, quebec-papa, eight-niner-niner..."

I ignore the radio banter and don't even look at my map. Fire missions aren't exciting to the Team anymore. They're just a thing, like villages and grape rows. They're just part of the environment. I'm having trouble staying awake.

The Sniper Sergeant thinks different. He is intent on listening to the radio and consults his own map. He notices something all of us miss completely. He whispers to the Officer, who quickly consults his own map. Oh geez, thinks the Officer.

A hand signal goes around our mixed platoon. It's an upward lifting hand followed by an axe motion to the east. Rise, people, rise and move out that way. No doubt Moses gave the same hand signal when he evaded the Pharaoh's Army.

We get up from our positions and walk eastward. The Officer gives a rapid milking-of-the-cow motion with his fist. Hurry!

I don't understand why it's so sudden. The smoke hasn't landed yet. We move, and move until we're a single file of soldiers again. I look behind and see that the last of our column is a hundred meters away from where we were.

Ka-Boom! Wump-wump-wump!

The sky splits above us with a fantastic sonic boom. The unseen shell tears apart into three fingers of grey smoke shooting into the ground as fast as bullets, making the weird "wump!" sound.

My vision follows one of the fingers of downward smoke into the piece of grape row I sat on previously. Another one hits the mud wall Brody used for cover.

Ka-boom! Wump-wump-wump!

The smoke shells, those thunderous claps breaking up in the air and shooting themselves into dirt, are landing where we were. The American Captain is giving the wrong Fire Mission. Fucking friendly fire. Thick clouds of grey obscure the village.

Ka-boom! Wump-wump-wump!

Amidst the smoke and dangerously falling metal pieces, I make out the huddled form of a woman clad in a blue burqa as she shepherds her children away from the awful ruckus. I make out a little girl in a village dress, too small to be running in a war, and I hear terrified screams from inside the smoke.

Oh God.

I look at Jasher wordlessly. I know what he's thinking. I can tell by the strain of worry on his face. Oh God, those poor kids.

The Sniper Sergeant stands to a side as the column walks by, "I knew something was fucked with that Fire Mission."

"Thanks, Hammy," I tell him. The man saves our lives from stupidly being hammered by sonic smoke shells, and all he gets is a thank you.

The column breaks away from the grape rows and farmer's fields of the village without further incident. The enemy becomes a no-show for the remainder of the day.

The Team never visits the village again, and I have no way to tell what damage those shells did to peoples' lives and homes.

It's dark and I spend the night curled up in the cold, open desert. I want to think on those kids, but my mind is too busy trying to stave off the cold. I need to fall asleep. I tell myself, "I'll sort it all out later," and I fall asleep.

Master Corporal Daniel Yun

Daniel Yun served as an armoured reconnaissance crewman with the Queen's York Ranger's 1st American Regiment (R.C.A.C.) from 2005-2014. He deployed to Kandahar, Afghanistan from 2010-2011 as a Weapon's and Tactics Instructor on Operation ATHENA with the 1st Battalion Royal 22nd Regiment Battle Group Roto 10. In his civilian life, he is a retired veteran and planning for a new career.

I volunteered to go to Afghanistan to gain operational experience in an active combat setting. At the end of November 2010, I was deployed under the 1st Battalion Royal 22nd Regiment Battle Group Roto 10 based out of CFB Valcartier, Quebec. My time and experience over in Afghanistan is something that I will never forget I took pride in serving my country and helping make a difference over there

Our main mission was to support the ANP (Afghanistan National Police) in terms of mentoring the police force and other ANSF (Afghanistan National Security Forces) so that they could successfully carry out their duties as law enforcement officers. I was based out of Forward Operating Base Walton which was located in Kandahar City, Afghanistan. The unit I was attached to was called Regional Training Centre-

Kandahar (RTC-K) also known as "Scorpion" which fell under the NATO Training Missions-Afghanistan (NTM-A). I was also employed as Weapon's and Tactic's Instructor while I was worked alongside my fellow Canadian and U.S. counterparts and collectively working towards achieving our mission.

The mentoring mission team was divided into two teams. The first was Tactic's team which was comprised of combat arm soldiers and the second was a body of military police and civilian police units from the Royal Canadian Mounted Police and Toronto police members. The team always remained vigilant in their duties and worked well cooperatively with the ANP forces even in the face of a combatant situations.

Upon my return back to Canada in the summer of August 2011 I had a very difficult time transitioning back to life at home and adjusting back to daily regular routines was not easy. There was an incident outside of the Forward Operating Base Walton on the ANP force's camp that resulted in the injury of one of our members. He was a Captain that we worked alongside with from the

Operational Mentor Liaison Team also known as OMLT. Despite that setback we all collectively had to persevere in the face of our many hardships and endure it together in order to successfully carry out our mission. One of the main things I will truly miss about my deployment is the true strength of our brotherhood bond that we all formed together through our experience over there. And of course, the leadership from FOB Walton that helped guide us through our difficult times there. To our U.S. counterparts we were known as "Walton Wranglers."

I know war is the best thing in the world and with it comes many ugly and difficult experiences to everyone who is caught up in the middle of it. But through this experience I have learned to be thankful for the important things that I have in my life and never to take things for granted. This experience has truly made me a different person in a more better positive way and I have learned to truly appreciate the difference we made over there together and hopefully made a lasting impact in the lives of the Afghans.

Master Corporal Andrew Siwy

Andrew Siwy served in the Regiment from 2001 to 2011. He deployed on two operational tours in Afghanistan, in 2006/7 and in 2009. In his civilian career, he is a firefighter with Vancouver Fire Rescue Services.

I joined the Regiment via the Co-op program in February of 2001 at a time when people still asked "Why do we need an Army". A few short weeks after the end of my first CAC in Petawawa that question was no longer asked. The events of 9/11 changed many lives and some more so than others. For me it changed everything. My current career as a Vancouver firefighter is because of the many small events that happened after 9/11 that steered me to a more exciting and fulfilling job than my job at the time as a plumber.

I first deployed in 2006, in an ATR (Any Trade Required) "fastball" mission. Unfortunately, I had just missed out on a driver position in Kabul. This was at a time when everyone was itching to go on tour and most (including myself) were not picky as to the job. My first tour was a great experience helping transform KAF into a comfortable place for troops to 'recharge their batteries' between patrols or stints in the various FOB's. I helped in the construction of the TOC, Canada House, and hospitals and even the detainee facility, of which I will speak about more in regards to my second tour.

After returning home and being laid off by my employer I did what any 22-year-old would do with a big bank account, I travelled. I visited WWI and WWII battle sites and many countries throughout Europe. That summer I accepted a summer task at Borden as the CQMS for the Cadet Training Centre in Blackdown. After that tasking I was hired back by my civilian employer. During this time, a very proud moment for me was when I was presented the General Campaign Star by the Regiment's Colonel-in-Chief, HRH Prince Andrew at Downsview during his visit to the Regiment.

In the late fall a 6-month tasking at CFS Alert in Nunavut came up. I had always wanted to visit or serve at the 'top of the world,' and as I would be in the Arctic for six long months, I applied and was accepted. About a month out from deploying, I decided to take a two-week trip to Japan. The day before I flew home I received an e-mail stating the tour had been cancelled as NDHQ had decided to hire civilian contractors instead. Needless to say, I was furious. Once I arrived back home I begged my employer to hire me back, which he did, but without giving me the raise he had promised if I didn't go to Alert.

That whole summer, all I could think about was deploying. I had a friend who worked in Brigade Ops and he told me that there was a CANSOF tour coming up and they needed 10 reservists. I thought "Why the hell would CANSOF need reservists...especially of any trade?" It turns out that since they were so busy conducting operations, they needed manpower to guard their facility in FOB Graceland. I had high hopes, and knew who to ask to best get my name up the chain as soon as possible—and I thought that a bottle of Havana Club probably wouldn't hurt either.

In October we were told that there would be a briefing at NDHQ for those that applied, and pending successful selection (phycological testing, physical fitness, etc.), I along with Sgt. Boulton would be accepted. Well this was half true, upon arriving at the Holiday Inn in Ottawa there were fourteen people for ten positions. Apparently, a few units sent more members than their allotment, hoping that that perhaps someone would be a "no show" and they would get the spot. I immediately figured they would be sent home, however the Sergeant Major said that we would now have a selection over a three-week period, and that by the end four people would be cut. This was very frustrating to hear, as I had submitted a leave of absence to my employer. But, I knew that hard work would pay off. One member was dropped for missing the PT standard on the first run (about 10km but we were not told how long the run would be). The other three were dropped as well for a variety of reasons, but overall it seemed that they just didn't "fit the mold."

Like all deployed troops, we were given ZAP number for casualty reporting, but in CANSOF this number is used for your ID instead of your name or service number wherever possible. When it came to giving my ZAP to me, the Sergeant Major said "Si..shie...shww...AH, FORGET IT, from now on you're 0041!"

When we arrived in Petawawa we received our new gear from CSOR, as we were attach-posted to them. We all walked out with a huge duffel bag (the size of four normal Canadian Forces issued ones) full of off-the-shelf tactical gear. Plate carriers, pouches, slings, holsters, IR lights, tourniquets, flex cuffs, you name it, we had it. As we attempted to put our plate carriers together, we asked one of the CSOR guys, "Where we should put each pouch?" He said, "Wherever you want." We smiled and tried to explain that we had no idea what was best—what would he recommend? He gave us the same answer! This definitely wasn't the conventional army.

Over the next four weeks, we were placed on the CANSOF Supporters Course. It was basically a toned-down version of selection with all the fun stuff included and without any of the physical or mental stress. We spent one whole week shooting our pistols, the Sig Sauer P226. It was such an awesome experience. We had three JTF2 members teach us how to shoot. However, by the end of that week we were so sick of loading magazines! We had gas mask training, map and compass, escape and evasion classes, and lessons on the C8, Carl-G, M-72, and shotgun. It was like all the fun times in the Army wrapped up into four weeks.

It was only after these four weeks were completed that we were called into the CSOR classroom and the Chief Clerk said "Okay I don't want to make a big deal about this, so I am just going to read the three names of guys who are going home, and then I am leaving." Tension filled the room, but when I didn't hear my name I was instantly relieved. Of course, there were no WOO HOO's! as the three members were also in the room... that would come later that night at the 'Great Canadian Warehouse.'

It was just before Christmas and although CANSOF had treated us as equals there was a pay problem for all of us. None of us had been paid for over a month and a half. Apparently it was a problem at NDHQ. The Chief Clerk said "Okay I know it is not the ideal solution, but if anyone needs a pay advance come downstairs and we will forward you $5000 CASH, no less. It is $5000 or nothing as the computer is down and I don't want to issue many differing amounts." Well, we all took it and hoped we would make it to the bank safely.

We were then on Christmas leave for the next thirty-six days, and I managed to catch a ride back to Toronto with Corporal Newton from the Governor General's Horse Guards. After he started the car, he told me that his heater had just conked out. We decided to make the trip anyway as Petawawa is not the most exciting place to be for thirty-six days in shacks, even though it was well below -30C! In Kaladar we stopped and looked for a plug-in heater, but there was nothing that would work. So, instead I bought three candles! It was a long cold drive that night. He dropped me off at home and 5 minutes later called me. I figured I had left some kit in his car, and so was surprised when he said: "Siwy you're not going to believe it... the heater just kicked on." I could not make this stuff up!

Five weeks later, we were back in Petawawa with one last week before deploying to get all the loose ends sorted out. On the last day of shooting there was a small blizzard, and we could barely shoot pistol as our hands were shaking so badly. At about 10 a.m. the Sergeant Major from

JTF2 said "That's it, this training isn't effective." After this serial, we are done for the day." Did I hear him right?! Too cold to train? He later told me, "What is the value of training with pistols in -30C weather, when next week we will be in Kandahar and we can shoot there at +30C?"

So, with all our gear packed (including the gear bought with our $700 civilian clothing allowance and beard trimmers— as were strongly encouraged to grow one), we flew out of Ottawa on a chartered plane, making a quick stop in Amsterdam and then Dubai. I was amazed to see the transformation of the Kandahar Airfield in the two short years since I had been there last. The bombed-out hanger looked new and there seemed to be less 'poo dust in the air' too. This was because they were halfway done paving all the dusty dirt roads on base.

We had a short stop and we were to be picked up by a Chinook around 4:30 p.m. The time passed slowly and I remember getting restless, thinking that we would miss seeing the surrounding areas by air with darkness at hand. Well the timing could not have been better. The Chinook had a 'sling load,' meaning that there was a hole in the middle of the floor and the ramp was left open. This provided us with an incredible view of the sun setting over the mountains. To this day, this was one of the most beautiful views I have ever witnessed.

We landed at dusk and got settled in. We had a two-week handover with our counterparts (all Naval Boarding Party types). They were a 'weird' bunch, but as they say, "if you can't say something nice then don't say it at all."

FOB Graceland is the CANSOF portion of the larger FOB Gecko, and the American SOF FOB was FOB Maholic. There were several rumours on why the name 'Graceland' was chosen—that a picture of Elvis that was found when it was set up, or that JTF2 had a love of the 'King's' music. I believe it was more because of the lavish conditions that were found there, such as the rose garden that was tended daily by a gardener, or that the mess served Perrier water, Hagen Daz ice cream and "Steak and Lobster" on Thursdays. Graceland had been the former home of Taliban Leader Mullah Omar. One of the caves they hid in after 9/11 was less then 800m from us, and on our FOB. We checked it out several times and it was very well built. It was a simple cross-shaped tunnel made of concrete through a hill with multiple rooms. Once a week we also got to climb the nearby mountain called "the Elephant," which provided amazing views of Kandahar City, including Kandahar University and its beautiful blue mosque, which was paid for by Osama bin Laden many years earlier. I was very happy and surprised to bump into Master Corpora. Chris Astley, a former Ranger, now working in Intelligence. He was just a few weeks away from the end of his stint, but it was great to see him.

On Sundays we had shooting practice with a wide variety of weapons—pistol, C8, grenade, M-72, shotgun, sniper rifle up to .50 calibre machinegun, FN C1, M-48, grenade launcher, AK-47, PKM, etc. We also learned how to drive off-road with our Humvees, which we used alongside our quad bikes.

Our main mission was defence and security of FOB Graceland. We inspected all vehicles coming on to the FOB and were the Quick Reaction Force in case of any attacks. We also provided security for any detainees taken during missions. Ironically, they were then sent to the detainee facility I helped build two years earlier.

Over the tour, we had several rocket attacks and shots fired at our FOB. On a return visit from KAF we were told our convoy was being watched and the enemy were planning an attack. We were not in LAVs but 'low vis' vehicles like Toyota Hilux, armoured only with bullet proof glass. Just as we neared Graceland, an ANA Soldier at a checkpoint didn't notice who we were (as we were in low vis vehicles and out after curfew) and aimed his AK47 at us and leaned it to take a sight picture. Being in the back seat there was nothing I could do, and even if I could he, was a good guy who had mistaken us for a potential threat, so I tucked my body in tight and hoped we would drive past without incident. Luckily the crew commander hit the police lights and siren that were hidden on our vehicle, and the ANA Soldier backed down and gave us a wave. That certainly got the adrenaline going. I jokingly said to the JTF2 crew commander, "Man, I hope you don't have any hard feelings by I curled up into a ball thinking that if he shot at us that you would take the rounds." He laughed and said "I would have done the same thing, there was nothing we could do except hope that he didn't fire."

In the weeks leading up to the end of our tour we started getting excited. Everyone began planning for our stop in Ibiza, which was where CANSOF decided to have their R&R location, instead of in Cyprus like the rest of the Canadian Forces. We actually got to vote on where we would like to stop. I remember one other option was the Canary Islands where my brother stopped after his tour with CSOR. I was also planning a six-week vacation in New Zealand and Australia. After a long tour, this would be an incredible experience and a great way to cap off an amazing year. We had our medals parade in theatre and were presented the South-West Asia Service Medal as we were under Operation Enduring Freedom and not the NATO led mission. General Vance (now the CDS) presented each of us with our medal and made sure to personally thank each of us as well.

All in all, it was an incredible tour and probably the most exciting time of my life. It was towards the end of my tour that Corporal Newton told me that he wanted to become a firefighter when we got home. This sparked my interest too, and after that last six months there was no way I could go back to a world of leaky faucets and disgruntled customers. Five years to the month after my tour ended, I received a conditional job offer with the Vancouver Fire & Rescue Services. Leaving the Rangers to move out west was the most difficult decision I had ever had to make. I have made so many lifelong friends in the Regiment, and many of them have molded me into the person I am today. I am so proud and thankful to have called myself a 'Ranger'.

Master Corporal Adam Dibiase

Adam Dibiase was a member of the Queen's York Rangers from 1997 to 2018. He served in Afghanistan on Operation ATHENA as the gunner in a Troop Leader's Coyote in Reconnaissance Squadron. In his civilian career, he owns a small business that rents and transports recreational vehicles.

In May of 2010 I was deployed to Afghanistan, attached to Recce Squadron of the Royal Canadian Dragoons as a gunner in one of the troop leader's call signs, working the 25mm Bushmaster on the Coyote. There were two fighting troops, an echelon and a squadron headquarters (SHQ) in the squadron, equipped with a mixture of Coyotes and LAV III Recce variants.

We spent a lot of our time—most of our time really—in overt observation posts (OP's), particularly three that were set up in Panjwayi District overlooking one of the main routes in and out of the area, which was a real hotbed of Taliban activity. Route Trixie was your typical Afghan road—dirt packed down until it was like concrete, with wheel ruts from all the traffic. But it was also one of the main routes in and out for our supply convoys and a prime target for Taliban Improvised Explosive Devices (IEDs).

The OP's were called Salavat, near a village just east of the main Forward Operating Base (FOB) at Masum Gar, Onya and Cliff. They were pretty bare minimum: just vehicle run up positions and some shell scrapes for us to sleep in. We'd be three hours on watch, then six resting or doing maintenance or whatever else needed to be done. We went for ten days at a stretch in each OP, then rotated back to the FOB for two days of rest, and then we were back out on the OP.

When I first got there, it was pretty hot during the day, but it cooled off pretty well at night. But that was the spring: by the height of summer, it was over 40 degrees Celsius in the day and not much better at night. And this was with us wearing our body armour, with tactical vests, ammo and everything else—all our battle rattle—so we were basically thirsty all the time. You had to drink a lot of water just to keep up with what you were sweating out every day.

We were watching Route Trixie pretty closely: looking to establish what the pattern of life was for the locals, what was normal and what was unusual—and maybe a sign of trouble. Most of the scenery was pretty typical for that part of Afghanistan, rows and rows of grape vines, a few mud brick grape-drying huts and a few low walls to separate one farmer's field from his neighbour's.

But mostly what we were looking for was people planting IEDs. Trixie was the main route running east-west from the biggest town in the Panjwayi to Masum Gar and our resupply convoys were running up and down the route pretty regularly. And just as regularly, they were finding IEDs on the route. We were watching it 24/7 and we couldn't figure out how they were planting these things in the road. There was one culvert in particular that was just littered with IEDs—almost every time call sign 4 (the battlegroup's combat engineers) went down that stretch of the route, they'd find something.

It was making us crazy: nobody could catch the guy who was setting all these IEDs. We sent out dismounted patrols to catch him in the act, but nothing. This went on for a couple of weeks, until one day a trooper in a Leopard II sitting up on the FOB at Masum Gar, which was on a hilltop that dominated the whole area, was testing out his sites and happened to look over in the direction of our culvert. There he sees a fighting age male, holding a shovel and skulking around the culvert we've been watching so closely.

They radio it in to us and sure enough, we can't even see the guy. So, the troop leader puts together a dismounted patrol and we race out to the culvert and catch the guy, detain him and take him back to the FOB. They ran the gunshot residue swabs over his hands, clothes, the shovel, everything and he lit up the test swabs like a Christmas tree—he had explosive residue all over him, even his shovel. I had taken the tactical questioning course, so I sat down and started asking him questions: who was he; what was he doing there; why did he have a shovel; all different angles into the same question: was he the one planting those IEDs? Every answer he gave was different: he couldn't keep his story straight at all, so clearly he was suspicious.

The Quick Reaction Force showed up not long after and took him back to the main base at Kandahar Airfield for questioning and we went back to the routine in the OP's. But before we did, we went out and found the blind spots this guy had been using to sneak his IEDs into that culvert. We sent out a dismounted patrol to walk around the area we were watching, playing "Can you see me now?" with the guys still on watch in the OP. It took a while, but we eventually found all the blind spots in our observation.

Three days later we got a report from the Intelligence branch confirming that our detainee had been the guy planting the IEDs. The engineers went through, clearing Route Trixie right after that and didn't find another IED in that culvert, and when they went through again the next day it was still clear. So, we'd gotten the right guy obviously.

On May 24, 2010 we were in OP Onya, and there was a massive explosion from the general direction of OP Cliff. There was a towering cloud of smoke and dust and the radio just lit up. "Contact IED!"

I had been off duty and asleep when the IED went off and it woke me up. We all just sat around the vehicles trying to figure out what had happened from all the radio traffic. We felt helpless. We were all worried because we knew all the guys in the call sign that had been hit; we all wanted to help, to do something, but there was nothing to be done.

That night, just after sunset, the OC of Recce Squadron came on the air and said he wanted everyone to put their radios on speaker, so the whole squadron could hear. Then he told us that it was his Zulu call sign that had been hit by the IED, during a resupply patrol to all the OP's, and that his driver Trooper Larry Rudd had been killed.

Chief Warrant Officer Dave Goldenberg

Dave Goldenberg joined the Regiment in 1992, and served as its Regimental Sergeant Major from 2012 to 2015. He deployed to Afghanistan as part of a Tactical Psychological Operations team in Task Force 3-06. In his civilian life, he is a police officer with Durham Regional Police.

I have to be honest, I was scared shitless my first day in country. We had done all the required training such as first aid, convoys, live fire shoots, and gun fighter, you name it we did it. During our training we would get regular SITREPs (situation reports) from the Battle Group that was currently in Afghanistan (TF1-06). In the latter months of their tour it was clear that they were in a shit show and were getting in TICs (troops in contact) regularly. Even though the news was not good and it was clear Canada was at war, it still seems far away. We had this "it's going to be different for us" mentality. I was feeling confident when I went on my pre-deployment leave that we were ready for what awaited us in Afghanistan. However, while on leave I received my first wakeup call which changed my feelings about the tour.

I was the second in command (2IC) of a Tactical Psychological Operation team (PSYOPS). The team consists of the commander, the 2IC and three NCMs (non-commissioned members), one of which was fellow Ranger, Cpl (Sgt) Matthew Wood. Our job was to deploy with the Battle Group, imbed in the Infantry Companies and assist their Commanders by providing insight into the Afghan culture. In addition, we were to assist in reinforcing local support for the Government of Afghanistan and The International Security Assistance Force (ISAF), and help to destabilize the enemy where possible. Based on our job description we had this unrealistic view that we would spend most of our time with the Company headquarters, but at the end of the day we were boots on the ground. This became very apparent on July 22 2006, before I had even left Canada.

On July 22nd, my family had a going away party for me in the backyard of my house. It was great, cold beer, thick steaks and good company. When the party was done and cleaned up, everyone had gone to bed except for me. I was enjoying the feeling of being a bit tipsy and was lying on the couch with my unrealistic thoughts of the adventure to come (telling myself everything would be ok). It was close to midnight when my cell phone rang, startling me. It was one of my fellow teammates, Peter. To the best of my recollections Peter said "have you heard the news". I had no idea what he was talking about. He then proceeded to tell me the horrifying news that a fellow PSYOSP soldier, one of the troops we would be replacing, had been killed by an Improvised Explosive Device (IED). Corporal Jason Patrick Warren had been killed and a two other soldiers from the team had been injured. They were out on a mission when the IED destroyed the armoured vehicle they were riding in. I was shocked, I didn't know what to say, all I could think was "what the fuck". Those few words spoken by Peter shattered the false sense of security I had created for myself and the team. This was real and in less than a week the team commander and I were heading over as an advance party.

I didn't tell my family the news and this wouldn't be the first time I would have to hold back information to keep them from worrying. I also decided that regardless of what my feelings were, I would not allow them to have an effect on the team. I felt it was my duty as a leader to ensure we maintained high level of moral.

On July 30 2006, myself and team commander, Captain Jason Demaine arrived at Kandahar Air Field (KAF), just outside of Kandahar City, Afghanistan. We were to start the handover process with the current Tac PSYOP team. I fought my fears the best I could by keeping busy, but it didn't help that on the first few nights at KAF we had two rocket attacks. In addition, the current team was still clearly in shock at the loss of their comrade.

Captain Demaine spent time with the other commander, while I was with my counterpart, Sgt Rob McCue. We had remained in touch throughout his time in Afghanistan and he would send me regular SITREPS. Rob always sounded upbeat and excited about what they had been doing. During the handover, he was trying his best to be as upbeat as he could, but he was not able to hide his concern for us. One of the things he said, which I will never forget, was when we were looking at a map of where his team had been during their deployment. He pointed at one area that they had spent a lot of time and where their Battle Group had the most difficulty. It was the Panjwayi District, which is south west of Kandahar City, in the Argandab river valley. He shared some of the stories of what had happened there, then looked at me with all seriousness and said, "whatever you do, stay out of Panjwayi". Not sure he realised it, but his ominous words would stick with me. However, I was powerless to act upon his warning as Panjwayi would prove to be unavoidable.

As August progressed, I started to feel better about my situation. We went on a few short missions to get our feet wet. Eventually a crazy thing started to happen, I felt better when I was outside the wire (off base). I was starting to enjoy sleeping under the stars out in the Afghanistan countryside.

On August 27th Captain Demaine and I were at the Tim Hortons in KAF getting our double doubles when the Battle Group Operations Officer (Ops O) stopped to have a chat. We took a seat on the steps near the Timmies and the Ops O gave us the basic outline of an upcoming operation (Op Medusa). He knew we had been trying to get out to do our PSYOPS job, but he needed us for other tasks on the Op. I can still clearly remember him saying, "sorry guys, I need every swinging dick on this one". We were first told that we would be deploying with Charles Company on the first phase of the Op, but that was later changed to "A" Company. In the end that change would prove to be potentially life-saving as the opening days of Op Medusa were unforgiving for Charles.

Before I continue let me take a moment to give a quick overview of what Op Medusa was, without getting too deep into the weeds. In the spring and summer months of 2006 the Taliban had made head way in the Arghandab River Valley, specifically the Panjwayi district. It is the same area that Mujahedeen had fought the Russians and won. Many Canadians may be surprised to know that this is a very fertile part of the country with crops such as grapes, Pomegranates, corn, cannabis and Poppies (opium) to mention a few. As beautiful as the area was, it was a nightmare to fight in due to mud vineyards, grape drying huts and other infrastructure. The Taliban had decided to make a stand in this area and had actual dug in defences. Canada had experienced stiff resistance and a large number of soldiers had be killed or wounded. Op Medusa was to be the response in order to push the Taliban out. It was the first major offensive for Canada since Korea.

We departed KAF on September 1st and moved to Patrol Base Wilson (PBW) which was north of Panjwayi, along Highway 1. Once there, we started to shake out and get up to speed on the overall situation. Soon we were given our first task, which was to secure the western flank on the Line of Departure (LOD) on highway 1. As there were only 5 in our team, I was tasked with convincing a section of Afghan National Police (ANP) to join us. Our mission was to set up a Traffic Control Point (TCP) at a crossroads approximately 3 to 4 km west of PBW and not allow any vehicles to travel east along the highway during the initial stage of the Op. It was a shit position as no matter what we did we were exposed to enemy fire. At the time we were in armoured G-Wagens and there was a "three vehicles" rule when travelling outside the wire.

However, for this mission we only had our gun truck, the Command and Control vehicle and whatever ANP pickup trucks that tagged along. Suicide Vehicle Born IED (SVBIED) were becoming more and more a threat. So, we set up some well-marked barbed wire across the road, approximately 100 meters away from our position. It acted as a line in the sand so to speak, it gave us some standoff and early warning in the case anyone tried break through. We placed our gun truck on the road as a physical barrier, and the Command and Control in some low ground on the side of the road. In addition to the C6 GPMG on the gun truck we had another which we set up in a dismounted position. This provided the best coverage as the threat was all around.

We felt confident on our first day (Sept 2) as we had a decent set up and had the ANP with us, who were good dealing with the locals. That day was filled with air and artillery attacks on Taliban positions. We did not receive any enemy fire that day. As the day wore on, with dusk approaching, I noticed the ANP starting to pack up their trucks. I spoke with their commander who told me they were leaving. When I asked why, his reply was "it's too dangerous here at night". No matter what we said about their obligations to stay, they packed up and left before dark. We didn't have the choice of leaving, we had a mission and there was no one else to assist us. That first night was relatively uneventful, but the air attacks continued. Through our night vision goggles we could see the Infrared spotlight from the Specter Gunship circling around the dug in Taliban positions. We ran our position similar to an OP (observation post), with two awake, one on the gun and the other on comms. The rest were trying to get some sleep.

On Sept 3rd the ground assault commenced, and we could see the LAVIIIs moving into position. However, that day ended with Charles Company being ambushed by the Taliban as they advanced to contact. During the ambush four Canadian soldiers were killed. As mentioned above, if plans had remained as originally stated, our team would have been attached to Charles Company during this phase.

On the morning of Sept 4th, while Charles Company was reconsolidating and preparing to continue with the mission, they were mistaken for a Taliban position and strafed by US A-10s. This left the Charles combat ineffective with one killed and many wounded. We observed the strafing and at first thought it was of Taliban positions and were cheering on the attack. Then over the radio we heard "check fire, check fire, check fire." This sad and unfortunate incident led to a reorganisation of units.

For the entire month of September our team had horseshoes up our asses. We were close but never received any direct fire or encountered any IEDs from the Taliban. For example, during the early days of OP Medusa there was Taliban radio chatter indicating increased activity in our area, however except for a couple rifle shots there was nothing of note. A few days in we were relieved at the TCP by a platoon from Bravo Company. No sooner had we arrived at PBW, a few km down the road, did the position get attacked by a Recoilless rifle. The attack caused some injuries and damage to a LAVIII, however the same attack on us would have been devastating with the vehicles we had. We would later return to the TCP and at one point acted as a cut off for Bravo Company as they engage targets close by.

Eventually, due to the reorganization of units, we were reassigned to a composite Company consisting of US Task Force Grizzly, remnants of Charles Company and 60. It was commanded by the American, Colonel Williams and he took our team under his wing. He called us his "Canadian Psyops guys." He actually employed us in the role that we had trained for. As a result, we were involved with the final push to Objective Rugby, which was the last stand for the local Taliban. Rangers were present when the Commander of Region Command South (RC South), Brig.-Gen. David Fraser came to Objective Rugby for a briefing by TF3-06 Commander, Lieutenant Colonel Lavoie. On September 17 Op Medusa ended and the battle group moved into other tasks.

On October 3rd our mission was finished, and we were instructed to return to KAF to prepare for new tasks. On this day, not only was our mission finished, so was our luck. Our entire team had a bad feeling that day because, as strange as it may sound, everything appeared to be going "TOO WELL". We jumped onto the first available convoy heading back to KAF and were just entering the outskirts of Kandahar City when we encountered a traffic jam. We all knew the longer we were in the jam the word would be spreading of our presence. This would give the Taliban time to set something up such as an ambush or IED. Eventually the traffic jam cleared, but then one of the trucks in the convoy experienced a mechanical issue...leading to more delays. Once that was dealt with, we started to move further into the city. As we passed what appeared to be a low-rise apartment building, a motorcycle on the side of the road made a move toward our Command and Control G-Wagen and it detonated just short of making contact. I was in our gun truck along with, Cpl (Sgt) Wood and our gunner, Cpl Chris Downy. All I remember is a huge "Hollywood style" ball of flame in front of us. At the time we were not sure if it was our other vehicle until we saw Captain Jason Demaine and his driver, Cpl Peter Bursev, running toward us. In the end the G-Wagen did its job with Jason and Peter only receiving some minor burns and ringing ears. If the bomber had waited a few more seconds, it could have been our gun truck that was hit with Chris perched in the turret. There were many acts of heroism during this incident by all involved, but that is a story all on its own. This event turned out to be the last day a G-Wagen was allowed outside of the wire. We eventually inherited a RG31 Nyala armoured vehicle from the TF3-06 RSM, the late CWO Bobby Girouard. It should be noted that later I found out that the driver who was dealing with the trucks mechanical issues was ex-Ranger, Corporal (later Master Corporal) John Nebel.

The above is only one small story out of all the experiences our team encounter during the tour. I can't express my thanks and appreciation to all the Ranger leaders through the years that prepared me for my tour in Afghanistan. Our team was a mixture of Armoured Recce and Infantry soldiers. Sgt Wood and I, both being Rangers, were in our element when working around the vehicles. Skills that I was taught by Rangers and employed in Afghanistan, were vehicle tactics, TCP, dismounted patrolling, Convoy escort, OPs and VIP escort (close security for CIMIC reconstruction teams). Along with our Infantry team members, this made us an effective self-contained unit. We were able to intergrade well with other units and organisation as we were competent, professional and didn't need to be babysat as was some other groups. All we ever asked for was to be included in planning, for some supplies and a place to lay our heads. This professionalism and effectiveness lead to our team being asked to patrol with US SOF units out of Sperwan Gar.

This was just a synopsis of our experiences and there are many other things that occurred. I am not sure if this will make any sense to anyone but me, but as I was writing this and reliving the events, it became apparent there were many other stories that are offshoots from this one experience.

Captain Corey Shelson

Corey Shelson joined the Canadian Forces Primary Reserve in 2002 as a Private with the Queen's York Rangers, and was commissioned in 2003 on transfer to the Regular Force. He deployed to Afghanistan in 2010 as 2 Troop Commander, 23 Field Squadron, 1 Royal Canadian Regiment Battle Group. He retired from the Canadian Forces in 2015, and runs a digital marketing firm.

Our troop had relocated from Bravo Company's area of operations at Strong Point SHOJA to the Oscar Company's area of operations at Strong Point FOLAD on 14 September. The planning for Operation "Matin Azem" took place from 13-20 September at Strong Point FOLAD. A lot of coordination was required because of all the moving parts in the plan and due to the complexity of the situation.

In Central and Eastern Panjwayi there were believed to be twenty different insurgent groups operating, each with a membership of five to ten insurgents. Having lost nearly every direct engagement they ever got into with us, their weapon of choice had become the improvised explosive device, or IED.

To my frustration, we'd been monitoring the Taliban as they dug in

IEDs across the area of operations all summer. I knew that our best chance at success would be to try and identify the locations of the IEDs before we deployed. In order to do this, I put in a request to get a list of all the "Intelligence, Surveillance, Target Acquisition and Reconnaissance" (ISTAR) reports in the previous three months along Routes Chester and Caribou that might be linked to IEDs. I received an excel file with about two hundred lines of data, and each line had a 10-figure grid reference and a description of what was observed. Now I am sure I could have put a request in for this information to be processed and plotted on a map through the geomatics cell, but I needed it quickly so I did it manually using mapping software that we had. I plotted every single observation onto the map, and once I did, the dozen or so clusters of activity were obvious. I used these clusters as the basis for our search, giving us a lot of insight into the real danger areas that we had to be aware of.

After issuing orders on 20 September, the troop and I were pretty confident that our plan was good and that we were mitigating risk wherever possible.

However, it was evident to all of us that we as the Engineers on the ground would have a vital and dangerous role in opening Route Caribou, Route Chester, Route Nightmare and Route Hellhound, four routes that had been shut down and not used through the summer fighting season due to the extreme IED threat. Everyone was well aware that months prior there had been multiple severe IED strikes which resulted in several soldiers being wounded.

Due to the high IED threat, Routes Chester and Caribou had been shut down entirely. From where we were in Strong Point SHOJA, we were actually able to watch the intersection of these two routes over the course of the summer using what was known as a Persistent Surveillance Suite (PSS)—a remote sensor suite hung beneath a tethered balloon. Through July and August, we would watch the Taliban dig in IEDs on a regular basis. Whenever we would see it happening we would do our best to engage them using mortars or an airstrike, but most of the time they would get in and get out so fast that we were too late. We would watch as a guy would run in and frantically dig a hole and then run back into the village. Twenty minutes later another guy would run back in and bury the jug of explosives and then run away as well. The next day we would spot a guy run in and hookup a pressure plate or string some command detonating wire, before running away as well. It was incredibly frustrating to watch, knowing that eventually some poor bastards were going to have to clear that intersection, and that in all likelihood it would be my troop.

As the commander of 2 Troop my mission was to provide close engineer support to allow Oscar Company to seize insurgent terrain and clear the intersection of Route Chester and Route Caribou and the village of Chalghowr. Oscar Company was commanded by Major Steve Brown.

Grouped with us were a troop of Leopard tanks (two with rollers, one with a plow), an armoured engineering vehicle (AEV) based on a Leopard chassis, a ZL front-end loader and three specialized road clearance vehicles – a Husky, Buffalo and Cougar.

The plan was to combine deliberate vital point search tactics and tank route proving and breaching capabilities to open the route as safely possible. Even still, the risk was still severe and as I thought about how the plan would unfold, I expected casualties. My troop had already lost three soldiers killed and a number wounded after five months in theatre.

At 0100 hours on 21 September, reconnaissance, snipers and an infantry platoon moved out ahead of us by foot, with an engineer detachment in support. Four hours later, I led our vehicles out of Strong Point FOLAD and along Route Caribou towards the initial objectives. Almost as soon as we had started, the convoy was halted. Our Husky had broken a metal detector panel, and it took thirty minutes for it to be strapped back on. As I waited in the heat, I could only shake my head and hope for better luck - every plan goes to shit the minute an operation starts.

After moving off again, we quickly reached the first location we planned to search, a dry culvert that ran under the road. Dismounted sappers, supported by an explosive detection dog, checked it out but found nothing. We mounted up again and moved farther east along Caribou.

I used the roller tanks to "prove" an area as clear of mins and IEDs for the company to use as a leaguer, and we got into position to be ready to support the infantry who were still moving dismounted up to the objective. I kept everyone mounted, and dropped down inside the shade of my vehicle to catch a cat nap. I'm not sure how long I slept, but I was awoken by a loud blast.

I got back up into the family hatch of my M113 and waited for the radio report of the casualties while coordinating with the AEV to plow a "combat road" through the open desert which separated us from Objective 4 where the IED had gone off.

Major Brown ordered the roller tanks to move east and prove a route to get an ambulance closer to the casualty. The roller tank took off cross country in the intended direction, but then inexplicably plowed into the four foot mud wall lining Route Caribou and started heading in the direction of the intersection that we knew was heavily infested with IEDs. Thankfully, a quick bit of direction on the radio got the roller tank reoriented and moving towards Objective 4 again.

Rather than wait for us to scrape a combat road, Major Brown began heading to the casualty in his LAV alone. While I understood the need to lead from the front, I contacted him by radio to try to get him to wait for the AEV. He refused, rolling through country that we knew was prone to IEDs, and we trundled in behind him instead, plowing a road for our return trip instead.

By this time we knew more about the casualty. An Afghan National Policeman had stepped on a pressure plate and had been severely injured in the left ankle. I was thankful it wasn't one of my guys, but still worried that on the first morning of a weeklong operation we'd already sustained a casualty.

I dismounted with my guys at the link up point and we cleared a safe lane with our metal detectors in the direction of where they would likely be moving the casualty from. Pretty soon, the stretcher bearers came around the corner, carrying the wounded policeman. His ankle was pretty mangled, but it was covered in dressings so I couldn't really see much of it. We moved the casualty to the ambulance and returned to the leaguer where a Black Hawk medical evacuation chopper landed and evacuated the casualty.

Within minutes of returning to the leaguer I was contacted by one of my engineer detachment commanders, who had found a second IED in the compound where the policeman had been injured.

Secondary, tertiary and even fourth and fifth IEDs had become routine by this time on our tour. A common Taliban tactic was to cluster their IEDs close together, as typically when one goes off there is a rush of troops to the scene to provide care to casualties. There had been a number of instances on our tour where these secondary and tertiary IEDs had caused additional casualties as we responded to the first one. By this point our standard operating procedure was for everyone to stop as soon as an IED went off until the entire area was cleared. We operated on the assumption that there were always more than one IED. It made casualty care and evacuation and very complicated thing to do, which was hard on morale. Simply put, the threat of secondary and tertiary strikes was fucking brutal.

They'd found a second pressure plate and power source, but couldn't find the main charge. Rather than move an EOD team to that location, he requested permission to blow it in place. I called my boss on the radio, and it took some convincing to get him to agree to just blow it rather than risk more casualties to get a team in there to exploit it. It took us two attempts to destroy the IED – the first one exposed the main charge, a four litre blue jug of an unknown bulk explosive.

By approximately 1100 hours that morning we had secured Objectives 4 and 5, and we were ready to start the clearance of the remainder of Route Caribou east to Route Chester. Pulling onto Caribou, we were hemmed in on both sides by four foot mud walls the entire length of the road. Picture walking down a single lane dirt road with four foot mud walls on both sides. The walls were about a foot thick.

I halted the lead tank just short of where the walls began and our lead section adopted their route opening posture with two individuals out on either side of the route so that they could observe the outside of the walls, in order to try and spot any form of wires, battery packs or hidden IEDs. We were supported by a low-flying Griffin helicopter which flew directly above us in order to scan for triggermen.

This section of the route opening was about five hundred metres long. We made it all the way to Objective 5 without finding anything. The combination of the vehicles on the road, the sweepers on each flank and the helicopter overhead may have seemed like overkill, but the area was known to have IEDs and this was the lowest risk way I could think of to clear it. We continued to employ this approach all the way along.

On the next leg of the route, we had a find.

Sergeant Drew Gilbert was leading the forward route opening section. Drew was unfortunately the only of the original section commanders in the troop who had not been killed on the tour. Sergeant Martin Goudreault (E32B Section Commander) and Sergeant Jimmy MacNeil (E32D Section Commander) had been killed by pressure plate IEDs while on dismounted patrols only fifteen days apart, on 6 and 21 June respectively.

I received a radio call from Drew: "Fuck. It happened again." About a month earlier Drew's section had found an IED that had been stepped on by one of us but had not gone off. It happened again, someone (we believe it was the contract dog handler) had stepped on the IED pressure plate but it had not gone off.

This time the IED was easily accessible so we called in EOD who took the time to fully exploit the IED, and as it was dismantled we realized why it hadn't gone off – one of the wires leading from the pressure plate was broken. The main charge was a twenty litre jug of homemade explosive buried underneath the pressure plate, more than enough to significantly damage a vehicle or wipe out my entire lead clearance section.

When the EOD team did a secondary search prior to blowing the main charge in place, they found a second device just ten metres away. We blew that one as well and, as it was getting close to night fall, I started to think about where to leaguer for the night.

I contemplated moving back to the previously established leaguer but I did not want to give up the precious ground we had taken that day. If we'd gone back to the first leaguer of the day, we'd have to clear this section of Caribou all over again. Five hundred metres doesn't sound like a long way, but with the IED threat in Afghanistan at the time, this was a significant span of terrain. I knew that if we moved back that route would have been IED'd in the night - there was no question, they would somehow sneak in right under our noses and get something in place.

I requested permission from Maj Brown to moved forward and secure the opposite side of Chester and Caribou intersection and establish a leaguer for the night. He approved my request and took off back to Strong Point FOLAD on a resupply run. I was essentially on my own to get everyone to the other side of the intersection and get everyone in a defensive position for the night that would allow us to keep eyes on the ground we had taken, and defend itself in the chance of a direct or indirect attached from the Taliban - both of which had become common over the course of the summer (machine gun, recoilless rifle, RPG and mortar attacks were occurring daily in our area of operations).

Talking to the tank troop leader, we decided to breach into the adjacent field with a roller tank and then scrape a combat road with the AEV for all the vehicles to use. It may seem counterintuitive but you need to remember, we were literally stacked up vehicle to vehicle on a four metre wide road flanked on both sides by mud walls, there was not room to manoeuvre vehicles around each other. We had to move in the order of march. Hence us not wanting to blow every IED we encountered - if we did we would literally have craters that would make the route impassable. So, I talked to the tank troop leader and we basically had a "professional debate" about how to get across the intersection. There were two options - either my guys and I walk across and open the route with metal detectors, or he rolls his sixty tonne tank with rollers across. Either way I was confident we would encounter an IED, but I felt like the lowest threat to life was to use rollers instead of trying to find them with metal detectors. He didn't love the idea, but it seemed like the best approach given the time we had before it was going to be dark out and we were stuck in place (there was no moving at night - far too risky given the IED situation)

We all took cover as the tank breached into the field, holding our breath. I 100% figured one of those rollers were going to strike and IED. He made it to the other side without incident. A few more vehicles rolled across the intersection in the proven path and the track plan for the leaguer was rolled. Eventually the AEV rolled up to me in the order of march and I had it scrape a twelve inch deep path across the intersection. It then scraped the entire track plan of the leaguer. The AEV then increased the defensiveness of the leaguer by plowing a defensive berm all around us.

As all of the vehicles rolled into the leaguer I took a couple of my guys and we grabbed our metal detectors and walked the track plan. It was a complete gong show. There were literally parts of IEDs plowed up in the spoils of the track plan that the AEV had plowed. To complicate the situation further, ramps of vehicles were starting to drop and guys were starting to barrel out of their vehicles to stretch their legs (let's remember that most guys had been mounted in their vehicles in fifty degree weather for sixteen hours by this point. There had been opportunities to dismount and stretch for some, but literally some people had been stuck in their vehicles all day. I got on the radio and ordered all ramps closed until we had a chance to clear the area around each vehicle. We counted several IEDs, a bunch of IED components and a bunch of jugs of homemade explosives in the spoils of the track plan. We worked with EOD to get the area cleaned up and allowed everyone to dismount for night routine. A strict track plan was established and defensive overwatch night routine put in place. We needed to keep eyes on these routes as best we could in order to prevent the Taliban from sneaking in an and emplacing IEDs in the night.

That night, I slept in my vehicle, monitoring the radio traffic. That was Day One, complete.

The next day we focused on clearing Route Chester down to Route Lake Effect and clearing the area that would become a forward operating base that we were tasked to construct upon completion of the clearance operation. I sent some of the vehicles ahead while the remainder of the troop conducted a deliberate clearance of the area around the intersection, just as we would do if clearing a minefield. It only took us thirty minutes to find a battery pack hidden behind a mud wall, and shortly after that, a main charge of a twenty litre and a ten litre jug. Another jug was spotted in the spoil from our plowing the night before. We also found a buried bag of medical supplies, and a weapons cache.

The cache included a brand-new 82 mm recoilless rifle round and a well maintained PKM machinegun and ammunition.

Major Brown arrived in our position and was very happy with the progress we had made, but wanted us to push on towards Panjshir. Around noon we had finished clearing the intersection. I left two engineer sections on site to begin laying out the camp boundaries and started the cut and fill heavy equipment operations to prepare the pad for construction. The remainder of my troop as well as the tanks and some infantry moved back to Strong Point FOLAD to resupply and from there moved to Panjshir.

When we arrived there, it was after 1400 hours, and we only had about four and a half hours of light left in the day. The original plan was for us to clear Route Nightmare south from Panjshir down to Route Hellhound in order to link up with an American Special Forces team who had been operating in the town of Chawlghor for the past forty-eight hours. They had been dropped in order to disrupt Taliban activity as we cleared Chester and Caribou. They had secured the area but could not walk out due to the severe IED threat along route Nightmare. Our troop was tasked to clear Route Nightmare from Strong Point Panjshir to Chawlghor, provide a safe route for the US SOF to walk out and a safe route for Canadian infantry to take up their position. We were then supposed to clear Route Hellhound west to the end of the road, a distance of about one kilometre, and obstacle it to help slow Taliban movement into the town. With daylight quickly fading I recommended to the Major that we breach a combat road with the AEV parallel to Nightmare, through a number of grape fields. This would get us in contact with the Special Forces team without trying to clear the IEDs that we knew were on Route Nightmare. It would also give me an opportunity to see the route with my own eyes before conducting the clearance operation the next day.

Major Brown bought into the plan, and so at about 1530 hours, I led us forward through the grape fields. The AEV made quick work of it and by 1600 hours. we had breached the combat road to Objective 8 and had linked up with the Special Forces. These guys were straight out of a Vietnam war movie. Some not wearing shirts, no helmets, half of them were wearing bandanas the other half in baseball caps. I spent about forty-five minutes talking to the EOD Operator in the Special Forces team, discussing the intelligence that they had received from local kids who said that no one would travel on Route Nightmare north of the intersection, as the Taliban had emplaced IEDs on that section of the road. He also told me that the kids had said that the grape fields we had breached were a no-go area as well. The most important and also the most terrifying piece of information I had received from him was that several of the pressure plates they had found were "no metal" or "low metal" content pressure plates. You see pressure plates were typically easy to find as they were typically made from metallic conductors such as saw blades, flattened tin, or other flexible metal that were held apart using spacers. You would think in 2010 we would have had some kind of technology to find these things but to be honest, the only way and also the most effective way to find these on dismounted routes was using a metal detector operated by one of my engineers. The problem with no-metal or low-metal content pressure plates is that they are very hard to pick up with a metal detector. There are a couple of reasons for this - the "no" / "low" metal content is in itself a problem as it does not cause the metal detector to make a sound. The other issue is that the routes themselves had a lot of metal content (garbage, buts, bolts, shrapnel, bullet casings, etc). Picture trying to find an IED in a landfill - yeah that was our job. Fuck me. We needed to come up with a plan to find these pressure plates.

Once I had gathered as much information as I could, I moved my vehicles back to Panjshir and briefed Major Brown on my plan. I wanted to use two teams of three men, one on each side of the road, to sweep visually and with metal detectors to try to find the power sources or wiring that led to the IEDs on the road. Without any significant metal parts in the pressure plate, none of our equipment could reliably find IEDs on the road itself without striking them. That being said, IEDs typically need a power source to function so the idea was to try and find the batteries which were most likely buried in the adjacent grape fields as opposed to looking for the IEDs on the route themselves. Once we had cleared the verges of the road, the rollers would be used on the route, followed by dismounted sappers walking in the tank tracks. The Major agreed, and by 1900 hours, I'd briefed the plan to my troop. We would step off at first light.

The next morning we started as planned, clearing from the far end of the route back towards the intersection. I hoped that this would give us an edge as we did the visual search, as we were approaching from the opposite direction they expected. I was lead on one of a pair of three man teams, and positioned myself along the extreme right-hand side of Route Nightmare.

We moved slowly and deliberately, checking all hits with the metal detectors very thoroughly. At times we would lay on our bellies in the grape rows and scan the road with our metal detectors, but we stayed off the route due to the extreme low/no metal content IED threat. After about two hours, we had cleared just a hundred meters of the road and the verges. We literally were moving inches at a time. Our patience paid off, however, when Cpl. Nathan Blanche reported that he had found two hidden wires, one black and one red. I halted the two teams and walked through the grape fields lining the right-hand side of the road to his location to have a look, finding a nine volt battery in the process. Fucking rights - we had found the pressure source as planned. The EOD team we brought forward to exploit the IED found a buried no-metal content pressure plate and a four litre jug of unknown bulk explosives. As they prepared to blow the IED in place, I reflected on the fact that the IED and its pressure plate was buried directly in line with the path that I had been walking, only about forty metres ahead of where I had been. Thank god for Blanche - he quite possibly saved my life that day.

To finish the job, I sent the roller tank down the route. To have 100% confidence in the route I asked for a volunteer driver from my troop and the two of us mounted up, dropped the plow on our Engineer variant of our LAV and scrapped a three inch deep cut off the top of the road all the way from Chawlghor to Panshjir. I wouldn't have been able to handle the guilt if we sent dismounted troops down that road and someone happened to step on something we'd missed.

By 1100 hours, the route was clear and open to traffic. We mounted up and returned to the intersection of Chester and Caribou and carried on with Phase 2 of the operation, which was to build a strong point that could house a platoon. Over the course of the next two weeks we found another dozen or so IEDs which included everything from buried explosives to buried artillery shells. On 22 September I got to go on leave home - I was one of the last from my troop to get to go - I had been in theatre six months and was ready for a break.

Overall, the mission was a success. Routes Caribou, Chester, Nightmare and Hellhound had been cleared, the village of Chawlghor was accessible again, and we had found and destroyed a large number of IEDs.

Most of all, though, I was happy that I managed to get through the operation without any of my guys being injured, and with no major issues. If I had to explain our success, I'd say it came down to three factors: the technical experience of my sappers, the slow and deliberate manner we conducted the operation, and the detailed planning we conducted prior to its execution.

Although my training was as a combat engineer, the foundation of what I knew as a soldier was learned as a Ranger.

Major Matt Lennox

Matt Lennox joined the Queen's York Rangers in 2002, commissioning in 2004. He served in Afghanistan as a headquarters watchkeeper in 2008. In his civilian career, he is a writer.

It is very widely known what sort of genteel and noble characteristics are embodied by an officer of the Queen's York Rangers. Indeed, a Ranger officer can be spotted from afar – and I dare say picked from a crowd – by his posture, steely gaze, dashing figure, and all-round air of "officerliness". His hair is roguishly long, his pinky finger is erect whilst imbibing of a beverage, and he knows just how sternly to squint his eyes when a situation becomes demanding. The question, naturally, is how the Ranger officer maintains his renowned character whilst embroiled in such overseas expeditions as your humble narrator currently finds himself; namely, volatile Kandahar Province in rugged Southern Afghanistan.

If I may, allow me to introduce you to the place I have called home for six months now: Kandahar Airfield – or KAF, as the plebes insist on abbreviating it. KAF is home to some 15,000 persons representing 88 national forces, including our own, as well as a host of police, political advisors, governmental employees, and private contractors. Bearing the population of a small city, KAF must naturally meet the minimal expectations of such, and so contains a number of comforts (I shall not bandy about the term "luxuries", as only our distinguished Captains Parkin and Stocker, stationed at Camp Nathan Smith, know the true meaning of the word luxury; when next you see them, do respectfully ask them how much work they accomplished between bouts of water polo in the "firefighting reservoir") with which one may think of home. Your narrator often finds himself striding along the boardwalk, cup of Tim Hortons coffee in hand (and pinky finger accordingly erect), surveying a ball hockey match.

When he feels he's had quite enough of the standard - issue mess hall meals, your Ranger officer can retire to the Dutch – operated Echoes restaurant. There has the opportunity to pay for food he could have gotten for free in the mess, but which is distinguished by being fractionally altered in its placement on the plate. Should he wish entertainment, our officer may visit the A/V section of the US PX, where there are 6,000 copies of the motion picture *Fool's Gold* available for purchase. Of course, the patient Ranger officer need only wait for the Saturday bazaar, where he can purchase a pirated copy of *Fool's Gold* for a mere fraction of the price, along with mats woven with the images of AK-47s (essential for the home or office), and any number of rusting Soviet helmets (essential for the mantelpiece).

Of course, no visit to Kandahar Province would be complete without a jaunt out of KAF and into the territories, as the insufferable Mr. Twain may call it. Kandahar City, needless to say, is a shambles, where life nevertheless goes on, from the open-air butchery on the corner, where the freshly skinned (and still dripping) flanks of lamb or goat are hanging, to the "open-concept" municipal sewage treatment program, to the colony of tent-dwelling nomads on the outskirts of town. The urban air has about it a certain je-ne-sais-quoi of automotive exhaust and burning rubbish, and one's ears are graced with a veritable acoustic layer-cake of car horns honking, afternoon prayers, and the odd burst of a Kalashnikov.

Beyond the city the Afghan countryside is a mix of barren desert and patches of dusty green agriculture, amidst which are set mud-walled compounds of the sort one imagines from one's no-doubt studious and frequent, not to mention Protestant, studies of the KJV. Ever-present on the horizon both far and near are the jagged spines of brown mountain ranges. Along the highways, one may frequently observe craters in the asphalt, refilled with gravel, which mark the places where the Enemy has previously detonated his homemade explosives. The Enemy favours culverts for the placement of these nefarious devices – a fact that is not lost on even the most stout-hearted of Ranger officers when it is his very own classically-featured visage peering into said culvert, verifying that the space is free of anything but sluggishly flowing mud and human refuse, and that the awe-inspiring personage of the Deputy Commander, whose merest wishes are your narrator's immediate commands, may proceed unimpaired.

Your narrator is happy to report that he is not alone in his adventuring here; I am often happy to bid a fond "Good morning, old chap!" to Major Bosso (the Camp Commandant), WO Atyeo (flying about in his laundry-laden Tata lorry), Sergeant Nemeth (aging gracefully, as one would expect), Master Corporals Russell and Balancio (on the rare occasion that they are in from the territories), and of course Captain Bateman and his Merry Men (always striking fear in the heart of the Enemy and foiling their attempts to molest our noble supply convoys). Captains Parkin and Stocker, as previously hinted, are met with only at such times as your narrator is able to go to them, as they are naturally reluctant to depart the holistic retreat known as Camp Nathan Smith. They do, however, wish me to pass on to you that they are "Keeping it real" – whatever that means!

Captain Ryerson Maybee

Ryerson Maybee joined the Regiment in 1994, commissioning in 2012. He has served on three overseas tours, twice to Bosnia and once to Afghanistan. In his civilian career, he is a security manager at the City of Mississauga.

We got up at 0300 hours and left our small combat outpost in downtown Kandahar city for the southwest end of the city. On the drive we passed the MiG aircraft at the big traffic circle near Sarapoza prison. We pulled into position just to the east of what once was Alexander the Great's palace when he came through here on his way to India.

I was in command of our small Operational Mentor and Liaison Team (OMLT) as my boss, a Captain, was on leave. We were ordered to mentor the Kandak S2 or what we would call the Battalion Intelligence Officer while he commands the operation. Our rifle company, the 4th, is part of the cordon and search that is looking for Taliban rumoured to be in the area. Our job was to put in a block with one platoon from the company and then the other two would sweep west to east. All was well until about 0700 hours when 2 Platoon got into a contact with an IED strike—we heard the boom at our little CP which consisted of our TLAV, RG 31, the Kandak's Ambulance, and an ANA Ford Ranger.

Immediately after the boom of the IED detonation we heard small arms and our interpreter reported the contact from Lt Zhorian and the Company Sergeant Major Nasir. Fortunately, there were no friendly casualties—but no confirmed enemy casualties either. The operation was called as "complete" just before noon, and we headed over to the assembly area where the National Directorate of Security (NDS), Afghan National Police (ANP), and their American mentors from 504 Military Police battalion all were. At about that time Colonel Sherzai of the ANP, who was the commander of all the police in Kandahar province at the time (if I recall correctly) approached me and asked if I had an engineer asset attached or available. Some of the NDS guys had uncovered a bunch of IED material and the Colonel wanted some assistance disposing of it. This presented some problems:

1.   I had exactly zero Engineers attached to me.

2.   The nearest Canadian ones belonged to the PRT Callsign 4 but were notoriously busy pretty much all the time.

3.   While we had excellent comms with the company and all of its platoons, they had no maps.

4.   Problem number 3 was less of a problem anyway as most ANA guys couldn't figure out a grid reference without a great deal of assistance.

Regardless, I reached out to C/S 4 to see if they could help and they promptly told me that their engineer assets were currently dealing with another IED and wouldn't be available for some time. No surprises there. I reported this to the good Colonel and suggested he ask his mentor for assistance, to which he replied "My mentor left".

Sure enough the American mentors had all left. After a bit of back and forth with Colonel Sherzai he determined that the best course of action was for him to head down to the site himself. Our Kandak

S2 had been pretty nonchalant throughout the operation, more interested in chatting and drinking tea with his mates than tracking the progress or position of 4th Company. So, in effect, we had left our Afghan brothers high and dry—no mentors, and not a lot of liaison either(less yours truly).

Maybe twenty minutes after the Colonel left for the site there was an enormous explosion—the radio came alive with reports of an IED strike and casualties. Seconds later another extremely loud explosion. Any Canadian soldier could tell you that was likely the friends of the initial blast casualties tripping a second device on their way to help the men wounded in the first explosion. I winced and my 2IC exchanged knowing glances. Maybe thirty seconds after the second detonation a third explosion was heard.

I silently willed the remaining Afghans to be still long enough for us to get them some help. While I reported this to my boss, my 2IC tapped my shoulder and pointed. The S2 and Kandak doctor had mounted up in the ambulance and were getting ready to go down to the strike site.

I had to stand in front of it and yell at the S2 that until we had some idea of what was actually happening down there, and where 'there' was, risking the Kandak's only ambulance was exceedingly stupid. He finally relented but instead of doing something productive began chain smoking and talking excitedly with the Kandak doctor. Our interpreter informed me that 4th Coy had a casualty and that there were more among the ANP and NDS, while trying to get a better idea of where they were it became clear that they were extracting casualties back to us. I grabbed my medic and told him we should expect between 4-8 blast casualties imminently. He was a young guy from Montreal and he cheerfully replied "Roger!" He hustled off to get things ready including the ambulance. Moments later an ANP Hilux truck came into view kicking up a rooster tail of dirt as it screamed down the road towards us. I yelled at my medic and he gave a firm thumbs up as we braced ourselves to deal with the casualties. I was in the midst of preparing a 9-liner medevac request when the Hilux sailed past our position and carried on back into Kandahar city proper. All of us Canadians looked at each other in surprise. I asked the S2 what that was about and he replied he didn't know. I decided at that point that I was now in command of the Kandak's operation. By radio we got some decent info—there had been at least 4 ANP and one of our Afghan Army guys in the first explosion. They were still trying to figure out exactly how many more had been killed or wounded. One thing was clear to me—ISAF had no clue where, or what exactly was happening at the site.

By this time, we'd moved to Police Sub Station (PSS) 6 where we linked up with Col Sherzai's G3 officer (Operations). He didn't have a good handle on the situation either but knew that the colonel was asking for help. I told him and the S2 that I was going down there to get eyes on and bring some clarity to the whole mess. I got on the radio to my OC and told him what I was going to do, and he expressly forbade it. He was worried that we would have a strike on the way in and worsen the situation.

I was furious. I made the case again over the radio that at the moment we were about as useful as a screen door on a submarine and that this sort of thing was exactly what we were here to sort out. The OC was adamant. My 2IC and looked at each other and he said "why don't I go down and you can say I left before you could tell me that we weren't allowed?" I laughed and said I was thinking of going anyway. In the end we obeyed orders and stayed put. It's probably the one decision I made in theatre that I regret.

Throughout this whole ordeal I had one of my guys continue to try and raise the CO of 504 MP Battalion who was Col Sherzai's mentor, all without success. Callsign "Zero", the control station for the whole of the Kandahar city battlespace was conspicuously absent from the radio and so was 504 MP. Three hours later the Lieutenant Colonel who was in command of 504 MP made it out to PSS 6. I immediately briefed him on the situation. There had been three IED strikes in close proximity, multiple casualties, Col Sherzai was on the scene, but we had no idea where exactly it was.

He turned to face me and was visibly shaken, a kind of stunned affect to his body language, and said "What do you think we should do?"

Now as a Senior NCO in the army officers ask you this question all the time. Almost all of the time they want to get your perspective, leverage your technical expertise, or your experience. They have a plan in mind—they just want some validation or another opinion to tweak their scheme. This was not that. This was an officer who genuinely did not know what to do. Fortunately for him, I had been in position for hours, stewing at our collective inaction and furious at my own.

"Sir. We need to push an ISAF element down to where we can see the site, and report accurately back so that we can push the resources required to aid our Afghan comrades, and we need to do it RIGHT NOW," I replied. He nodded, turned away and headed over to his vehicle. I thought at last we were going to do something, but instead he dithered and seemed to do nothing. I pestered him twice more before it was made clear that I was no longer welcome.

I updated my OC and repeated my request to move to the strike site, which was immediately denied. Almost two hours more elapsed and a Blackhawk touched down nearby. A section of American infantry in mirrored ballistic glasses and in arrowhead formation approached, well spread out and clearly willing to engage *anyone* who looked like a threat, regardless of the uniform they might be wearing. At their centre was a tall heavyset man who shuffled the way old football players who had knee injuries do. He was armed only with a pistol. As he got closer I could see the subdued eagle emblem of his rank: a full colonel. His security detail flowed past me and the MP Lieutenant Colonel enveloping us as Callsign "Fury 6" shuffled up to us. He glanced at me quickly and then motioned at the MP Lieutenant Colonel. The MP gave a summary of his understanding of the situation that was rambling and disjointed, but had the gist. I hovered at the periphery the way you do at a house party when you're trying elbow into a conversation. Finally, Fury 6 looked me in the eyes and said "you're the OMLT guy".

"Yes, sir I am the OMLT guy"

"What do you think we should do?"

This was the question phrased the way I was used to hearing it, from an officer who had a plan in mind, but was looking for some additional perspective.

"Sir, we need to get down to the strike site immediately and assess the situation so we can support the ANSF with whatever assets they may need."

He nodded and turned back to the MP Lieutenant Colonel.

"Colonel you need to push some assets down to the strike site immediately to assess the situation and support the ANSF with whatever the situation calls for." The MP Lieutenant Colonel nodded and said "yessir". With that Fury 6 and his detail turned on their heels and headed back to the waiting Blackhawk.

Just as the MP was marshalling some vehicles to head down Colonel Sherzai came over the radio saying he was withdrawing the remaining forces due to Taliban ICOM radio chatter and the coming darkness. The dusty and exhausted 4th Company soon appeared and we mounted up and headed back to Old Corps, our base. I never was able to raise callsign "Zero." The whole mess had taken fifteen hours. When I got back to our Command Post, the OC debriefed my 2IC and I. We went over the whole day's events one more time and I expressed my disappointment and frustration at being held to the PSS. He congratulated us on a job well done and acknowledged my frustration, it was his call and he was ok with the decision. I shrugged and respected that stance. Then he said: "You guys want to know why callsign "Zero" was off air all day?" My 2IC and I looked at each other, then back at the OC.

"Yes sir, we do."

"They were moving the physical command post in the PRT base, and they didn't use a step up."

I laughed a deep belly laugh that can only come with the recognition of an absurdity. To put this in civilian terms, imagine that the 911 call centre for the city of Toronto went off the air without telling anyone for a whole day. Not due to enemy action, or some sort of criminal act, or natural disaster, but because they were moving buildings. The 504th MP battalion had recently assumed control of the battlespace in Kandahar city, and along with it came responsibility for callsign

"Zero," the city's command post. Apparently, the physical space that command post occupied was not to the Commander of the MP battalions liking and he wanted to use a different space at Camp Nathan Smith, the home of the PRT. The day he picked to move was one when two-thirds of the ANSF present in the city were conducting a major cordon and search operation in the south end of the city, a known Taliban stronghold, told no one and didn't have an alternate means for the CP to communicate with anyone.

In conversation with Sgt Major Nasir and the 4th Company's commander it was clear that Colonel Sherzai had maneuvered outside of the operations "box." One of the NDS guys had found a bunch of IED materials and to celebrate he and his team sat beneath a tree eating watermelon. When they had finished he picked up four jugs of homemade explosive, about twenty kilos, and walked over to his truck intending to secure the material. On the way he stepped on a pressure plate IED and was instantly vaporized. As the Company commander put it: "We did not find one teaspoon of him."

In that blast we lost one of the privates from the 4th and four ANP officers. As I had suspected, the second blast was another pressure plate triggered by people responding to the first one. Predictably the third blast was the same thing. My boss had given the OC of 4th Company a handheld Garmin GPS just before he went on leave and I asked to borrow it. I downloaded the map trace and finally figured out where the strike had happened. On radio watch that night I looked up the location in our secure intelligence database and not 300 metres from the strike site was a confirmed Taliban shura location. It looked to me like the good Colonel had stumbled into the defensive IED belt protecting that site and the nearby IED cache the NDS man had found. I was proud of my team and how they'd performed under the pressure, but angry at how impotent I was. It was our best/worst day of the tour thus far, but little did I know that there was more to come.

War in Iraq

In 2014, the Islamic State of Iraq and the Levant (ISIL) made rapid gains in both Iraq and Syria, prompting an international response. Canada, along with eight other nations, committed to fight ISIL in conjunction with Iraqi forces. Canada's commitment included headquarters staff, strike aircraft, special operations forces and trainers for the Iraqi army. By the end of 2017, ISIL did not control any territory in Iraq, and by March of 2019, their last territory in Syria was retaken.

Captain Chris Wattie

Chris Wattie was commissioned as a Second
Lieutenant in the Governor General's Horse Guards
in 2004, transferring to the Queen's York Rangers in
2008. He was deployed to Iraq on Operation Impact
as Task Force Information Operations officer from
July 2017 to March 2018. In his civilian career, he is
a writer and journalist.

There were nearly 500 officers and NCMs
in the Coalition Joint Task Force
headquarters for Operation Inherent
Resolve (CJTF-OIR), the multi-nation
fight against ISIS in Iraq and Syria, most
of them US Army or Marines. But there
was a healthy contingent from most of the
69-nations participating in operations
against ISIS, including about a dozen
Canadian staff officers.

The headquarters was situated on an
otherwise desolate stretch of Kuwaiti sand
and dust known as Camp Arifjan,
originally built as home base for two U.S.
Army Brigade Combat Teams permanently
posted to Kuwait after it was overrun by
Iraq in the 1991 Gulf War. The CJTF
headquarters occupied only a small corner
of the sprawling base, centred around two
tank garages converted into offices for the
staff and an enormous Joint Operations

Centre (JOC) – a vast open space organized like an amphitheatre around three Jumbotron sized screens showing everything from the latest news feed from Al Jazeera to sitrep slides from the various formations and units in the field. The centre screen was almost always set to a tactical map, a computer graphic of Iraq, Syria and neighbouring nations showing friendly (and other) units' locations and actions in lines and boxes that looked like a 1980s video game.

The JOC was the heart of the task force operations: from here the Commanding General (a three-star U.S. Army general), his deputies and chief of staff could monitor goings-on in the area of operations and pass orders through the various duty officers sitting behind desks and monitors lined up in a semicircle around the JOC. The JOC was a busy place during a major operation, but even in slow periods there was a fairly steady traffic of staff officers in and out of the room. This was largely due to the air conditioning. Temperatures in Kuwait and Iraq can top 50 C during the summer, and because of its concentration of computers, the JOC had the best air conditioning in the building.

The undisputed ruler of the JOC was the CHOPS, or Chief of Operations. On my tour, the CHOPS was a US Army colonel with a buzz cut, the physique of an MMA fighter, and a wickedly mischievous sense of humour. And during one particularly busy week in the JOC, he had noticed something odd. Two or three times a day, one of the Turkish officers on staff seemed to always be in the JOC, spending some time watching the tactical map.

The official motto of CJTF-OIR was "Many Nations: One Mission" but unofficially, the motto was "One Mission: Many Classifications." Almost every file we touched was classified and the levels of classification – and who was therefore allowed to read the files – ran into the dozens. The classification levels left some NATO allies in the headquarters feeling somewhat left out: the French contingent named two tame cats wandering around the Coalition compound attached to the headquarters NOFORN (the classification meaning for U.S. eyes only) and FIVE EYES (for the inner circle of Five Eyes nations: U.S., U.K., Canada, Australia and New Zealand).

Nobody felt this more acutely than the small Turkish contingent: about five officers working in various branches of the headquarters. During the three-year campaign against ISIS, Turkey had become deeply involved in the murky and multifaceted civil war in Syria; growing increasingly cozy with Vladimir Putin's Russia, more and more autocratic, and impatient with some of the anti-Assad rebel groups holding territory just over their border with Syria, particularly the Kurdish PKK which they considered a terrorist organization. In early 2018, this culminated in the Turkish army and its Syrian proxy forces invading the border city of Afrin with Turkish President Recep Erdogan declaring that he was prepared to go much further. In the words of one British general at the headquarters: "Turkey is not being a particularly helpful member of the coalition."

As a result, the Turkish officers at the headquarters were put in a sort of classification purgatory – their access to much of the operational planning severely restricted. That left the officers in their contingent with not much to do – in fact, the Turks seemed to split their time between the smoking area and the espresso machine just outside JOC. But they still had access to the JOC, and their routine of regularly checking on the tactical map made the CHOPS suspicious that what they were actually doing was gathering intelligence on CJTF-OIR to pass along to Ankara.

So, he decided to test his theory.

I happened to be in the JOC when his test went into effect, talking to my friend Dave, a USMC staff officer in the planning cell about an upcoming briefing. He quickly shushed me and urged me to sit down on one of the chairs beside his terminal. "You've got to see this," he whispered, nodding towards the tactical map on the main display.

What I saw on the black and green map display didn't make any sense. It showed a flow of Iraqi army battalions, with accompanying US and coalition support elements, moving north towards the Iraq-Turkish border close to the Syrian border.

"What the actual fuck is that?" I asked him. "Is there an op going on?"

I happened to know from a planning session I'd attended that afternoon that most of the units currently crawling northwards on the screen were supposed to be preparing to clear one of ISIS's remaining areas of control in western Iraq.

"Not exactly," Dave said, pointing quickly towards the JOC floor in front of the big screen. "Check out the Turk."

A Turkish lieutenant colonel was staring up at the screen wide-eyed from the floor. His mouth wasn't exactly hanging open, but he clearly hadn't expected what he was now seeing on the map. He recovered quickly – to his credit – and after a quick look around the JOC to see who was watching he managed to do a reasonable impression of casually strolling out of the room.

Dave chuckled and explained what the CHOPS had done. The colonel had created a test file for the tactical map program – originally designed to run operational simulations to exercise brigade or divisional staffs – showing almost every coalition, allied and US unit in Iraq beginning to march on Turkey.

A few minutes after the Turkish colonel left, the screen flickered and the real map filled the screen, showing the current position of all those units – sitting exactly where they were supposed to be.

"Now stick around and watch what happens," Dave said with a grin.

About 20 minutes after the lieutenant colonel had left the JOC, there was a flurry of activity on the screen. Turkish army units had begun to move in all directions, but mostly towards positions near the border.

"Looks like we ruined somebody's day off," Dave said cheerfully, watching southeastern Turkey erupt in a beehive of military activity.

The CHOPS just gave a sly smile and went back to working at his terminal.

SUPPORT THE REGIMENT

The Regimental Council of the Queen's York Rangers is a registered charity that raises funds to support the soldiers of the Regiment ant to preserve its heritage. You can find out more about the Regimental Council, including how to donate, at:

www.qyrang.ca

Made in the USA
Middletown, DE
14 September 2019